Violence In the Workplace

Education, Prevention & Mitigation

David Fowler
Founder and Author of
Workplace Violence Training Programs

AVADE®
Workplace Violence Prevention

Violence in the Workplace:
Education, Prevention & Mitigation

Published by Personal Safety Training, Inc.
P.O. Box 2957, Coeur d' Alene, ID 83816 (208) 664-5551

ISBN 978-0-9826163-2-1

Disclaimer

Neither the author nor the publisher, Personal Safety Training, Inc., do not dictate policies or procedures for the use of any violence prevention, self-defense or any physical intervention authorized for use by a department/agency or private individual. The suggestions/options disseminated in this book are simply that, suggestions or options. Each individual, department or agency is responsible for developing their own "policies and procedures" regarding the use of violence prevention, self-defense and physical intervention for their personnel and for themselves. Although every effort has been made for this book to be complete and accurate, it is impossible to predict, discuss or plan for every circumstance or situation which might arise in the course of defending yourself and any contact with a violent or aggressive person(s) or during a crime. Every reader must always take into consideration their experience, physical abilities, professional responsibilities, agency and department procedures and state, local and federal legal requirements. With this in mind, each reader must evaluate the recommendations and techniques contained in this book and decide for himself (herself) which should be used and under what circumstances. Each reader assumes risk of loss, injury, and damages associated with this book and use of the information obtained in it. The author and publisher, Personal Safety Training, Inc., cannot guarantee or warrant the legal, medical, tactical or technical suggestions/options in this book.

Any implied warranties are expressly disavowed.

DEDICATION

To all employees in every industry:

May the information on the pages of this book be more than just ink and letters. I pray that the strategies and techniques for dealing with violence and aggression in the workplace will be useful, practical and perhaps, even lifesaving. I hope you do more than just read these pages. I would encourage you to create new personal safety and self-defense habits and modify any existing limiting habits. This understanding of human nature, and knowing that "we are what we repeatedly do" will take you to the highest level of personal safety and success in your professional and personal life. And finally, my wish is that you share what you learn in *Violence in the Workplace*. By sharing, you will truly learn, and you will apply this knowledge for the safety of yourself and of others.

To YOUR Safety

David Fowler

David Fowler

ACKNOWLEDGEMENTS

First and foremost, I would like to thank God.

I would also like to thank the many teachers, instructors, mentors and friends who have helped make this book a reality. Without your help, inspiration and invaluable knowledge, this book wouldn't have been possible. To all of you, I am eternally grateful.

I would also like to thank the thousands of individuals whom I have worked with, whose direct and indirect contributions to this book have made it possible for me to do what I feel on purpose to do.

Special thanks to the following individuals for their support and technical advice: Mark Costello, Genelle Fowler, Brian Goodwin, Doug Kearns, Brian Keltz, Mark Loudin, Mark Mooring and Steve Pettillo. Your wisdom and inspiration echoes through these pages.

Very special thanks to my editor, Theresa Renner. Your grace, patience and wordsmithing expertise has allowed me to help others.

I would also like to thank my family for their support through this process: My mom, Nancy; daughters, Kaley, Hannah and Jacquelyn; sons, Shane and Aaron; and all of my extended family.

And finally, a most heartfelt thanks to my wife, Genelle Fowler. Your commitment, grace, honor, kindness, gentleness and most all, Love, has made all of this possible. ILYWAMH.

CONTENTS

CONTENTS

INTRODUCTION

Incidents of Workplace Violence happen every second, minute and hour of each day in the United States. OSHA and the CDC have declared that workplace violence is now an epidemic in some industries. Hospitals, government, law enforcement and corporate security continue to tighten down, but there are steps YOU can take, as an individual, to protect yourself from violence while on the job.

The AVADE® Workplace Violence Prevention Training was researched and developed as the most complete workplace violence prevention-training program available. It is based on research from OSHA, FBI, ASIS, CDC, NIOSH, BLS, State Workplace Violence Laws, Department of Labor & Industries, the Department of Justice, and more.... AVADE® Workplace Violence Prevention Training is an integral piece of an effective plan to prevent and mitigate violence in the workplace.

The Principles in the AVADE® Training programs stand for:

A = Awareness
V = Vigilance
A = Avoidance
D = Defense
E= Escape/Environment

An employer's overall plan should include administrative, behavioral and environmental strategies to prevent and mitigate the risk of workplace violence. The AVADE® training course provides this level of education and will also empower you to:

- Identify risk factors
- Recognize emerging situations before they turn violent
- Deal with an agitated or dangerous individual
- De-escalate individuals who are stressed, intoxicated, angry or combative
- Escape and survive a workplace violence incident
- Respond appropriately to an emergent situation

The AVADE® philosophy incorporates learning new habits, skills and actions that employers and employees can use to enhance their personal safety and their ability to defend themselves or others from dangerous situations, crime and violence.

AVADE® has been taught in private corporations, healthcare agencies, schools, community programs, and civic institutions for many years. The founder of the AVADE® Training programs, David Fowler, has over thirty years' experience and has made personal safety training his life's work. He has an extensive background in training, martial science, and all functions of security management and operations. He is also the author of *Be Safe Not Sorry: The Art and Science of Keeping You and Your Family Safe from Crime and Violence*, available on amazon.com and at his websites:

www.personalsafetytraining.com and **www.avadetraining.com.**

"The overall vision and philosophy of the AVADE® Training program is the moral essence of life itself, to live a safe and positive life with peace, security, harmony and freedom of choice."

Benefits of AVADE® Workplace Violence Prevention Training

- Increased Awareness
- Increased Confidence
- Increased Overall Safety
- Increased Quality of Life
- Increased Self-Improvement
- Increased Sense of Overall Peace
- Increased Ability to Protect Others

You will also experience:

- Reduced Fear
- Reduced Stress
- Reduced Injuries
- Reduced Liability Risk
- Reduced Loss of Property
- Reduced Feelings of Inadequacy
- Reduced Inability to Respond to Situations

If you have been through an AVADE® Workplace Violence Prevention Training program, refer back to this book as a personal refresher course. This textbook on workplace violence will teach you how to recognize emerging situations, how to deal with someone before they become violent, and how to survive and escape a violent attack and much more.

Read carefully. Integrate the lessons you learn here. Unfortunately, one day you may be responsible for saving your own life—and the lives of your co-workers.

Chapter 1

Some Hard Truths and Hard Facts about Workplace Violence

"Workplace violence" is a broad term. Not long ago, even a fist fight between co-workers in a parking lot was unusual. Unfortunately, in this day and age, we have seen a sharp rise in the escalation of violence from disgruntled and/or mentally ill employees, former employees, and customers/clients.

The National Institute for Occupational Safety and Health Administration (NIOSH) and the Occupational Safety and Health Administration (OSHA) define workplace violence as any physical assault, threatening behavior or verbal abuse occurring in the workplace. Violence includes overt and covert behaviors ranging in aggressiveness from verbal harassment to murder.

For educational purposes, we will expand on that. AVADE® defines workplace violence as:

Any act of aggression, verbal assault, physical assault, or threatening behavior that occurs in the workplace environment and causes physical or emotional harm to guests, staff or visitors.

Have you already been a victim of, or seen someone victimized by workplace violence? Workplace violence includes any of the following:

- Verbal harassment (name-calling, use of swear words, demeaning comments, etc.)
- Intimidation or bullying
- Obscene phone calls
- Property damage to work space or personal property, including your car
- Robbery
- A bomb threat
- Verbal assault (verbal threat of physical violence; i.e., "I'm going to kill you!")
- Witnessing a suicide
- A situation where a person just wouldn't leave you (or another) alone
- Road rage
- Gang violence
- A physical assault, where you or someone else was
    - pushed, shoved, spit-on, grabbed, kicked or slapped
    - taken hostage
    - kidnapped
    - threatened or attacked with an edged weapon or a gun
    - sexually assault

Workplace Violence Statistics[1]

- Almost 2 million employees suffer non-fatal workplace assaults every year.
- Homicide is the fourth-leading cause of fatal occupational injury in the US.
- Homicide is the leading cause of workplace death for females.
- Most non-fatal workplace assaults occur in the service industry, typically by the guest/client.
- 50% of non-fatal injuries to workers from assaults and violent acts occur in social service settings.

[1] According to the US Bureau of Labor Statistics, http://www.bls.gov

Workplace Shootings[2]

- In the years 2004 - 2008, 564 work-related homicides occurred each year in the US (10% of all fatal work injuries).
- 4 out of 5 victims were male. Assailants were both men and women.
- Shootings accounted for 80% of all homicides in 2008 (421 fatal injuries).
- Co-workers and former co-workers were the assailants in 12% of all shootings.
- Robbers were the assailants in another 40% of cases.
- Nearly half of the shootings (48%) occurred in public buildings.
- Most shootings (86%) occurred in the private sector.
- 14% of shootings occurred in government.

Workplace violence can be devastating to deal with. If you have suffered any of the above, you may need to seek some type of assistance (Employee Assistance Program and see Bibliography for additional resources). Learning and integrating the AVADE® techniques in the training course and in this book will help ensure that you know what to look for. This will reduce the chances of YOU becoming a victim of workplace violence.

The Myths of Workplace Violence

[2] According to the US Bureau of Labor Statistics
http://www.bls.gov/iif/oshwc/cfoi/osar0014.htm

There are several dangerous myths about workplace violence. Knowing the truth will help you to be better prepared if you ever face an incident of workplace violence.

Myth #1: That would never happen where I work.

In the early 1990s, the phrase "going postal" entered the American lexicon, after eleven post office shootings left thirty-five people dead between 1983 and 1993[3]. Contrary to that slang term, however, workplace violence is not confined to post offices, or *any* one industry. Workplace Violence can happen at any place of employment with social services and healthcare being the highest in non-fatal assaults against employees.

There also seems to be a misconception that workplace violence is a uniquely American phenomenon. But incidents of workplace violence have occurred in Europe, Asia, South Africa, Canada, Australia and New Zealand. It can happen anytime, anywhere. Anywhere there is a workplace, incidents can happen. Learning the AVADE® principles will help keep you, and others stay safe.

---

[3] Vick, Karl, "Violence at work tied to loss of esteem", St. Petersburg Times, Dec 17, 1993

Myth #2: There's nothing you can do about it. People just snap. You can't predict it.

This is, perhaps, the most dangerous myth about workplace violence. Do a little research on almost ANY incident of workplace violence and you will quickly see that the perpetrator gave warning signals. In virtually *every case,* there were signs that the violent person was escalating and about to perpetrate a crime. The only caveat to this is that we don't always have the opportunity to see the signs. A person may just walk into your place of business and go off. Healthcare, law enforcement and the security industries are more prevalent to this, as their work is based on emergent needs.

Prevention is the key to creating a safe and friendly environment for guests and visitors, as well as a safer workplace for staff. It is possible to prevent and reduce the effects of violence. The most important step is to establish a comprehensive program in the workplace, dedicated to educating, preventing, mitigating, tracking incidents, and providing support for those affected.

Myth #3: My employer doesn't care.

Employers *do* understand the risks and do care. Many employers are adopting policies and procedures for preventing workplace violence. Aside from the human cost, workplace violence costs businesses a lot of money.[4]

- The cost to US business from workplace violence is estimated at more than $120 billion a year.
- Costs of non-fatal workplace assaults: 876,000 lost work days per year, $16 million in lost wages per year.
- The average jury award, in subsequent liability cases where the employer failed to take proactive, preventive measures

[4] http://www.bls.gov/

under OSHA guidelines, is $3.1 million per person, per incident.

Currently, there is no federal standard that requires workplace violence protections. However, The Occupational Safety and Health Act of 1970 (OSH Act) mandates that, in addition to compliance with hazard-specific standards, all employers have a general duty to provide their employees with a workplace free from recognized hazards likely to cause death or serious physical harm.

OSHA will rely on Section 5a-1 of the OSH Act, the "General Duty Clause," for enforcement authority. Failure to implement these guidelines is not in itself a violation of the General Duty Clause; however, employers can be cited for violating the General Duty Clause if there is a recognized hazard of workplace violence in their establishments and they do nothing to prevent or abate it. These standards address employee safety and security risks.[5]

Recently (September 2011) OSHA announced a new directive targeting workplace violence prevention. In this directive, OSHA is actively investigating and citing employers for failure to keep their workplace safe from threats and incidents of workplace violence.

Some states have sought legislative solutions, including mandatory establishment of a comprehensive prevention program for employers and employees.

If you are reading this book and have *not* gone through AVADE® Workplace Violence Prevention Training, ask your employer if they have adopted policies and procedures and response training for preventing workplace violence. If not, request to have AVADE® training. At the very least, read and re-read this book. Ultimately, your

[5] http://www.osha.gov/Publications/OSHA3148/osha3148.html

safety is YOUR responsibility, but your employer may simply not know what's available as training for you and your co-workers.

Chapter 2

Creating an Effective Workplace Violence Prevention Plan

There are three categories of an effective Workplace Violence Prevention Plan:

- Administrative
- Behavioural
- Environmental

The AVADE® Workplace Violence Prevention system is designed to give you the training and education you'll need in the prevention and mitigation of violence in the workplace. Agencies must also consider and implement the appropriate administrative, behavioral and environmental categories for developing protocols and procedures for their workplace violence prevention plan.

Administrative Protocols and Procedures

There are many components to the administrative policies, practices and procedures for a successful Workplace Violence Prevention system.

Workplace Violence Prevention Policy: The importance of a comprehensive policy that strictly prohibits violence and threats against the workplace, as well as other behaviors deemed inappropriate is the foundation of preventing violence in the workplace.

No reprisal reporting policy: It's vital to create an atmosphere where employees feel safe in reporting strange, threatening or abusive behavior. If employees fear reprisal, people in authority may never know that an employee, client or guest is behaving in a threatening manner. Some employers have instituted anonymous caller lines, where employees can leave information and keep their anonymity.

Documentation and record keeping: Documentation is essential in reducing the liability an agency could be exposed to. If an employee needs to be let go, or a client or guest needs to be barred from the premises, documentation of inappropriate behavior will be necessary for legal purposes. Proper documentation also allows companies to mitigate certain areas that have been identified through tracking and trending.

Incident reporting procedures/structures: Many states require that all workplace incidents/injuries be reported to the department of Labor and Industries or other regulatory agencies. Proper reporting structures must be in place for managers and supervisors. Employees need to be trained to identify and report incidents that could be indicative of an emerging problem.

Security management prevention plan: A security management plan helps employers identify risk factors and risk areas. Once identified, a well-trained security manager and team can respond to, and more importantly, prevent situations from escalating to violence. This proactive response planning identifies potential risk factors with strategies to prevent, reduce and eliminate risks to staff, clients and guests.

Management commitment and employee involvement: AVADE® training has many components. From basic employee awareness training to more advanced training. We recognize that security, management, supervisors, human resources personnel and department directors play a unique role in workplace violence prevention and will need more tools. Using the AVADE® training and principles, everyone in an organization can participate in keeping the workplace safe. Overall, to successfully prevent and mitigate workplace violence the commitment must come from the top down. It is essential to get leadership buy-in.

Emergency code procedures and response: Chapter 13 discusses some common emergent situations that happen in all industries. Things as simple as knowing where your exits are, knowing how to dial 911 out from a company line, and knowing where alarm buttons are can save lives. Proper training in emergency codes and response is critical.

Departmental risk level assessment: Certain risk factors help us identify if a department is a low, medium or high risk. Department managers must also have the training to identify potentially dangerous situations and know the procedures for responding to and reporting them. Many companies utilize the security management plan to help identify risk factors in all departments and work areas.

Workplace Violence Program evaluation: Knowing that workplace violence is a three pronged process—administrative, behavioral, environmental—is essential to the program. An employer's overall program should be reviewed periodically to ensure its effectiveness. As the environment changes in the workplace, so will the plan needed to reduce potential risks.

Human Resources: Human resources play an integral role in the development and implementation of a successful workplace violence prevention, mitigation and intervention plan. Policy development, staff training, incident tracking and reporting, union negotiations, departmental coordination efforts and disciplinary actions to enforce policies are key components in which human resources involvement is necessary.

Human Resources hiring and termination protocols and procedures: With consistent, careful pre-employment background checks, many problems can be averted. Termination procedures should be handled correctly and consistently by trained individuals who understand the potential risk factors and warning signs of workplace violence.

Legal Counsel: Using in-house legal counsel or an outside firm for an understanding of the legal obligations related to workplace violence is essential to an organization.

Threat Assessment Team: A threat assessment team is a group of individuals, usually comprised of security management, human resources, department heads, administration and others. This team evaluates the risk factors of an individual with warning signs who has been recently disciplined, terminated or is being investigated for workplace violence. The team collaborates and determines the best course of action. During high-risk assessments, a clinical psychologist specializing in workplace violence may need to be retained from an established reputable consulting firm.

Staffing levels: Particularly in retail and health care settings, it's vital that sufficient personnel are present for the safety of employees. The old saying holds true, "there is safety in numbers."

Behavioral Training

Training and Education: AVADE® Workplace Violence Prevention training is, perhaps, the most important component in a Workplace Violence Prevention Program. Understanding risk factors and what constitutes potentially dangerous behavior, and how to deal with it, is the first line of defense against workplace violence.

Post Incident response procedures: If a workplace violence incident DOES occur, policies and procedures need to be in place *beforehand* so that employees have a clear course of action and know what to do. See chapter 8 for information on how to respond after an incident has occurred.

Post incident reporting procedures: For legal protection of yourself, your co-workers, and your company, proper post-incident reporting is essential. Post follow up to incidents can help reduce and even eliminate re-occurrence if action steps are taken.

Self-Defense and appropriate Use of Force: We all have the right to defend ourselves. Proper training and education in self-defense techniques and an understanding of the appropriate use of force has reduced injury, saved lives and reduced liability exposure. Certain industries will need comprehensive training on controlling and restraining individuals. Healthcare, security, law enforcement and behavioral health typically need additional training in this category, as their jobs are at higher risk.

Environmental

Creating a physically safe environment for employees has been shown to minimize threats to employees, guests and clients/customers. Rather than industrial concerns (such as ensuring heavy equipment is safe to use), here we're talking about environmental components that promote and support the Workplace Violence Prevention Program. See chapter 12 for information on the environmental tools in your environments that can help keep you safe.

Worksite audit/analysis: This is similar to a security management plan but specific to all areas of the workplace and anywhere employees are. Many employers use audits and analysis of workplace violence incidents to help identify, prevent and mitigate risk. An environmental analysis would include checking in areas outside of a workplace, where someone could hide out in shrubbery etc.

Panic alarms: Proper placement of panic alarms for high-risk areas and staff education on using them is essential. Do you know where your panic alarms are? Do you even have panic alarms? If so, do you know how to use one and what happens after it has been activated?

Access controls: Door locks and security devices on doors are designed to keep people out and are only as good as the people using them. Proped doors, piggy backing and access numbers written above the lock fail to ensure a safe work area.

Physical Lighting: Criminals don't like lights! Things as simple as ensuring there are no broken/unusable lights in bathrooms, dark hallways and parking lots can keep people safe from a violent incident and reduce crime.

CPTED = Crime Prevention through Environmental Design: This concept is gaining ground around the world. CPTED promotes things such as lighting, ensuring pedestrian routes are open and visible, and even minimizing shrubbery in vulnerable places so that assailants have no place to hide. Many corporations utilize CPTED in pre-design and new construction. It can also be utilized in environmental security audits and analysis as well as the security management plan.

AVADE® Workplace Violence Prevention Objectives

AVADE® principles and learning objectives are integrated throughout the Administrative, Behavioral, and Environmental components of an effective Workplace Violence Prevention Plan.

1. **Awareness:** Your Workplace Violence Prevention Plan will increase your overall awareness of worker risks to violence, and

provide strategies to prevent and mitigate these risks.

2. Vigilance: Understand the characteristics of violence and the predicting factors related to it.

3. Avoidance: Reduce and eliminate incidents of workplace violence through administrative, behavioral and environmental protocols and procedures.

4. Interpersonal Communications: Understanding the assault cycle and developing skills to de-escalate the different types of aggressive behaviors are important factors in mitigating workplace violence.

5. Defense of Self and Others: Mitigate liability risk through proper documentation and the understanding of using force to defend yourself or others.

6. Stress Management: Provide methods of team debriefing, post-incident response, and techniques for dealing with daily stressors.

7. Time & Distance: Increase understanding of reactionary response to a physical or weapon assault situation.

8. Escape Planning: Pre-planning escape routes from all environments and learning physical maneuvers and positioning to prevent isolation and assaultive situations.

9. Environmental Factors: Understand appropriate safety techniques and departmental systems and procedures for the different areas of the workplace.

10. Emergency Codes and Procedures: Provide and increase awareness of the agencies protocols and procedures for responding to an emergent situation.

All of the AVADE® components, learning objectives, principles, skills and training techniques are what is needed to create an effective Workplace Violence Prevention Plan.

Chapter 3

Proactive Response Planning= Prevention and Intervention

Proactive vs. Reactive

Prevention and intervention are essential to eliminating and mitigating security risks in the workplace. Employers now recognize the importance of being proactive in their implementation of workplace violence policies and procedures, conducting work site audits/analysis, tracking and trending incidents, training and educating staff, as well as other proactive measures to reduce the risk of violence to guests, staff, clients and visitors. A well-thought-out plan for the prevention of workplace violence takes on a proactive response versus an after-the-fact, reactive-driven response.

General Personal Safety Measures

MIND, BODY, SPIRIT and ENVIRONMENT—General personal safety measures involve maintaining a balance and awareness in all areas of your life: mental, physical, spiritual and your environments.

Personal Safety & Self-Defense Habits

"We are what we repeatedly do;
therefore, excellence is not an act, it is a habit."

- Aristotle, Greek Philosopher

Habits are our acquired patterns of behavior that occur automatically without thought, things we repeatedly do over and over. They can be either good or bad.

We Are Creatures of Habit

You get up in the morning a certain way and get ready for your day. You brush your teeth, comb your hair, put on your clothes, etc., the same way, every day. You don't even think about it; you just do it. The way you answer the phone, greet people, shake hands, gesture, smile or not smile are also all your habits.

Habits are ingrained in you and stamped into your unconscious mind.

"Sow an act and you reap a habit. Sow a habit and you reap a character. Sow a character and you reap a destiny."

-Charles Reade, English Novelist, (1814-1884)

Habits are powerful factors in our lives. They are consistent, unconscious patterns that constantly and daily express our character and produce our effectiveness—or ineffectiveness. Habits determine your future and your safety!

Developing Personal Safety Habits

Identify Your Limiting Personal Safety Habits

Do you have habits that leave you unsafe? Such as leaving your car unlocked, or working late and cutting through unlit areas? Take a hard look at your daily habits and see what little things you can do to ensure your own safety. Once identified, you can begin to change and improve them.

The 21 Rule

This is the process of making small adjustments in your behavior. Twenty-one days of repeatedly doing what you intend to do, to create a new habit. The 21 Rule is not applicable to a habit that we have had for an extended time. Long-term habits have roots like trees and run very deep. Changing or eliminating long-term habits could take as long as a year or more to develop or break.

Creating New Habits

Write out your new personal safety habits. Once you identify your limiting and successful habits, you can clearly decide to change them, or make new, more productive and empowering personal safety habits. Having a clear, defined personal safety goal is the first powerful step to creating a new habit.

Take Action with Visualization

Written words are powerful—but only when you look at them and make an effort and a commitment to follow through. Focus on your new personal safety habits often; focus on the benefits of your new habits. Use the process of visualization to add more repetitions to your successful new habit. More on this in the next chapter when we discuss using mental movies.

The No Retreat, No Surrender Policy

The no-surrender policy means that you will do whatever it takes to change or accomplish your personal safety goal. This policy is about doing it even when you don't feel like it—when you're tired, sick, hungry or stressed. You do it no matter what; you make the commitment!

Evaluate Yourself and Ask for Help

Ask yourself, could I do more to improve my general personal safety and overall sense of safety? Ask for help and get more training. A good trainer will gladly let you know the areas that you could improve upon. Look to improve in all the areas that you received negative feedback, too. Negative feedback is not necessarily "bad." Consider negative feedback as a way to add safety and self-improvement to your personal life. It's about taking responsibility for yourself and your circumstances.

If you change or add one new, empowering habit every other month, in five years you will have thirty new habits. Remember, habits are something we unconsciously do—once they're ingrained, you don't even have to think about them.

Chapter 4

Increase Your Awareness

"Awareness is the power that is concealed within the present moment... The ultimate purpose of human existence, which is to say, your purpose, is to bring that power into this world."

- Eckhart Tolle, *A New Earth: Awakening to Your Life's Purpose*

Everything in life begins with *awareness*. Have you ever said this to yourself, "I would have done that if I had been of aware it." The goal of this chapter is to help you understand what awareness is and how you can increase yours. There are many levels of awareness, and we will briefly look at them and why they are important to your safety in the workplace.

Awareness is defined as: *A mental state or ability to perceive, feel or be conscious of people, emotions, conditions, events, objects, and patterns.* The key to awareness is knowledge and understanding. The gift of this awareness is wisdom.

Change your awareness and you can change your life!

Increase your Awareness of Worker Risks to Workplace Violence

- **Lack of staff training in recognition and de-escalation of workplace risks**
  - The biggest risk is not recognizing that an individual is escalating and not knowing how to avoid the situation or how to use your interpersonal communication skills to de-escalate that person.

- **Working alone or in isolated areas**
  - When working alone, remember to increase your 360 view of awareness to keep yourself safe. Practice what police officers do when dealing with a person in conflict, get back-up!

- **Not using or having electronic safety measures**
  - Electronic safety measures (alarms, access controls etc…) are only as good as the people using them. Know and understand how the safety controls in your environment work. If not sure, as questions—get training.

- **Contact with prisoners and the mentally ill**
  - Some industries have a higher prevalence of contact with these individuals. However, any of us can be exposed to mentally ill consumers and ex-inmates. Be aware and have a plan.

- **Low staffing levels and increased consumer waiting**
  - It's a fact of life in our current economy; we are all expected to do more with less. This means our consumers may have to wait for our services or products. Use interpersonal communication skills when dealing with consumers who are upset.

- **An increase and prevalence of weapons in society**
  - Weapons are everywhere; they can be everyday common tools we use at work. Increase you awareness of what is around you and how it may be used as a weapon to inflict harm. Guns and knives are not the only threat we face today.

- **Presence of gang members & high crime areas**
  - Demographics of where we live, commute and work are factors that predispose us to crime and violence. Be aware of these potential areas of risk and avoid them if possible.

- **Access to pharmaceuticals/drug seekers**
  - One thing is for certain, people will continue to seek and use drugs. Working with pharmaceuticals can put you at risk. Increased awareness is needed for industries that prescribe or administer drugs.

- **Drug and alcohol use among consumers**
  - Working with people who are under the influence of

alcohol or prescribed and non-prescribed drugs may expose a person to an increased risk.

- **Distraught family members and visitors**
  - Stressed indivuals may escalate into higher levels of the assault cycle. Recognizing that a person is distraught can increase your ability to de-escalate them.

- **Handling of money/transactions**
  - Anytime you work with valuables or money there is an increase in risk. Assaults and robberies take place daily due to the fact that certain individuals will commit crimes to get those assets.

- **Public Access (often 24/7)**
  Any workplace that is open to the public around the clock exposes employees to certain risks. An increase of criminal behavior occurs more often during certain times of the day than at others times.

- **Late and early work hours**
  - When workers arrive or leave work during late night or early hours it may expose them to an increased risk of workplace violence. Workers are encouraged to get security escorts if available and travel to and from parking areas with co-workers.

- **Home care visits**
  - Entering into another person's residence may leave a person vulnerable. Certain precautions and training should take place to equip personnel on what to look for and how to respond when providing home care visits.

Self-Awareness

This conscious awareness allows you to think, reason, choose and exercise free will, evaluate options and make decisions. Through your self-awareness you have communication with your body through the sensations of sight, sound, smell, taste and touch. You are using your self-awareness right now as you look at these words, decipher their meaning, think about the message and make decisions of its validity.

"Every human has four endowments—self-awareness, conscience, independent will, and creative imagination. These give us the ultimate human freedom... the power to choose, to respond, to change."

- Stephen R. Covey, *The 7 Habits of Highly Effective People*

Emotional Awareness

Your ability to recognize and feel the emotions and feelings of others, as well as your own, is your emotional awareness. When you are aware and in control of your emotions you can communicate with compassion and empathy. When you are emotionally aware, you also recognize the patterns and changes in others around you. This ability to know that the behavior of a co-worker or a regular client has changed can give you the opportunity to intervene, report your concerns or distance yourself from the individual.

Emotions are "the glue" connecting people to one another. They are the foundation of our ability to understand ourselves and relate to others. When you are aware and in control of your emotions, you can think clearly and creatively; manage stress and challenges; communicate well with others; and display trust, empathy, compassion and confidence.

When we lose control of our emotions, we spin into confusion, isolation, and doubt. By learning to recognize, manage, and deal with your emotions, you'll enjoy greater happiness, health and better relationships.

Your emotions help you:

- Understand yourself, including your deeply-felt needs
- Understand and empathize with others
- Communicate clearly and effectively
- Make decisions based on the things that are most important to you
- Get motivated and take action to meet goals
- Build strong, healthy relationships

Understanding the emotions in others as well as yourself helps you evaluate the behaviors of others and how you are feeling about a person's behaviors. How does all this relate to your safety in the workplace? Simple: trust your feelings/emotions. If a situation or someone in particular is raising your level of fear or anxiety, trust that feeling and take the appropriate actions.

Situational Awareness

Situational awareness means being aware of what is happening around you. It means understanding how information, incidents, and your own actions will affect your goals and objectives, both now and in the future. Lacking situational awareness or having inadequate situational awareness has been identified as one of the primary factors in accidents attributed to human error.

It is best explained in a simple equation:

I + R = O
Incident + Response = Outcome

If an employee or customer is angry and escalating (incident) and knowing how to respond (response) to the situation can lead to a non-violent outcome.

By taking responsibility for all the situations you are in, you can increase your personal safety by making conscious, informed choices and decisions about your environments, the people around you and the places you frequent.

Environmental Awareness

Environmental awareness is the ability to understand and recognize the many factors relating to your environment and how they can benefit you or limit you. It also means having an understanding that your external physical conditions can affect and influence your growth, development, and physical survival.

Creating an awareness of what is around you at all times is described as a 360-degree environmental awareness.[6]

Unconscious Awareness

Unconscious awareness is the part of the mind that directs the involuntary and automatic processes of the body. Through its operation, it automatically rebuilds, repairs and operates your body. Your unconscious awareness is the storehouse of your memory, habits, beliefs, instincts, emotions and knowledge. In chapter 3 we discussed the importance of personal safety habits. Knowing that habits reside in this part of our awareness gives us the opportunity to program our automatic responses by using the mental movie techniques to create personal safety habits.

Mental Movies and Impressing the Unconscious Mind

As humans we have the ability to pre-play events in our mind. We also have the ability to re-play past events in our mind. Most people have experienced both facets of playing mental movies and impress-

[6] The concept of creating a 360-view and awareness was created by Mark Mooring of Proper Authorities.

ing the non-conscious mind. Unfortunately, most people spend far more energy pre-playing negative events (worry) and re-playing negative events (past events that were negative) than visualizing positive outcomes.

Make a conscious choice to pre-play events to your liking and re-play positive events.

Here is how we impress the unconscious mind so that we can respond automatically without having to stop and think about what we need to do. A preplanned response can literally save your life.

Stage 1: Create the scene of the event, incident or situation in your mind's eye.

Stage 2: Make the scene as clear and colorful as possible. Focus your mind's eye as you create this clear concise mental scene.

Stage 3: "Lights, Focus, Camera and Action!" Now that the scene is clear and focused, give it action. As the director of your mental movie you direct everything in it.

Stage 4: The plot/outcome is up to you! You decide what happens, when it happens and who it happens to. You are the hero of your mental movie. You always win in your mind's eye when you create, direct and choreograph the mental movie.

Stage 5: Feel what it is like to be the star of your mental movie. Positive energy helps build, reinforce and utilize the mental power we all have. This ultimately makes us stronger, more decisive and automatic in our responses.

Stage 6: Remember to pre-play your mental movie prior to situations happening. We are the only creature with this ability. Re-play positive outcomes and try not to re-play negative outcomes of real situations. If you do re-play negative situations in your mind's eye make sure to always change the outcome to your choosing.

Higher Awareness

Many, if not most, people believe in some form of an infinite and eternal energy from which all things proceed. It is the reality that underlies all existence and is everywhere present. This state of awareness is the highest, as it encompasses all the levels of your awareness as well as your spiritual/energetic awareness. Some people call this awareness a sixth sense, and many people have credited it with keeping them out of dangerous situations, or even saving their lives.

Constant Communication

Our self-awareness, emotional awareness, situational awareness, environmental awareness, unconscious awareness and higher awareness are in a constant state of communication with each other. Even though we are not cognizant of this, it is continuously present. Just knowing this is the beginning of increased awareness.

Developing & Increasing Awareness

Developing and increasing your awareness does *not* mean becoming paranoid or hyper-vigilant. It simply means using all your senses to be aware of what is going on around you.

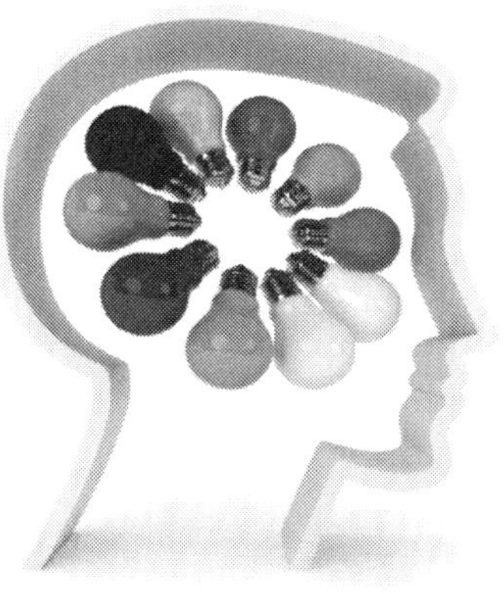

There are several ways to improve and increase your awareness.

1. Planning and preparing for situations that haven't happened yet. This is done by pre-playing (mental movies) what you would do if faced with a crisis situation.

2. Being Responsible or **"Response-able"** is the ability to choose your awareness, responses and attitude towards incidents, yourself and others.

3. Pay Attention to what is going on inside of you and outside of you.

4. Be Present. You don't have to keep your mind constantly busy thinking about all the possible things that can go amiss. Be present—

or in the moment—allows your awareness to be at its most optimal state.

5. Be Proactive. Recognize the importance of responsibility and awareness. Proactive people don't blame circumstances or conditions for their behavior or outcomes. Their behavior and outcomes are a product of their own conscious choices, based on their knowledge and values rather than their circumstances.

6. Attitude Is Everything. Your success with everything you do depends on your attitude. Creating a positive attitude about life and all of the events you will experience will help develop and enhance your awareness.

Make small commitments and keep them.
Be a light, not a judge. Be a model, not a critic.
Be part of the solution, not part of the problem.

Chapter 5

Vigilance

"We can never relax our vigilance about crime,
about enforcement, about prevention...
there's going to be some new problem down the road."

- Janet Reno, the first woman Attorney General of the U.S.

What is Vigilance?

Vigilance is the practice of paying attention to our internal and external messages with regards to ourselves, other people, things and events.

NOTE: Hypervigilance is a negative condition of maintaining an abnormal awareness of environmental stimuli that causes anxiety, leads to exhaustion and causes us to startle easily. Hypervigilance is counter-productive and unhealthy. Learning the AVADE® principles will give you the tools you need to live a happy, safe life without allowing fear to consume you.

The five senses: touch, smell, hearing, taste and sight, are the mental connection through our bodies to the outer world. Our senses can also alert us and keep us safe from danger. Many people believe that there is a sixth sense.

Trust Your Intuition

Intuition is knowing without knowing why. Intuition communicates with us through symbols, feelings, and emotions. It's like radar for sensing, seeing or feeling danger before it is present.

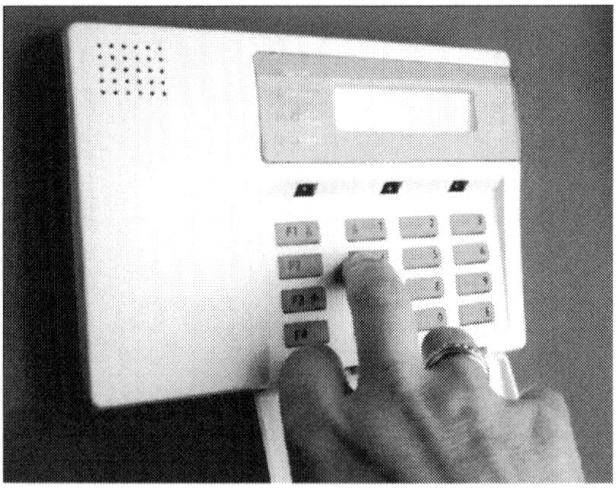

"All great men are gifted with intuition. They know without reasoning or analysis, what they need to know."

-Alexis Carrel, French Biologist and Noble Prize Winner, 1912

Intuition is a personal security system that is always on and ever vigilant, surveying not only danger, but everything else as well. *Trust your intuition.*

"We need to be willing to let our intuition guide us, and then be willing to follow that guidance directly and fearlessly."

-Shakti Gawain, author

Using Your Intuition

The ability to read a person's attitudes and thoughts by their behaviors was the original communication system used by humans prior to spoken language. In his book, *Body Talk: The Meaning of Human Gestures*, author Desmond Morris lists more than fifty body signals (messages) that are universal to all human beings in every culture. The majority of these messages are communicated unconsciously. Just as the communication is unconscious, so is our ability to read this non-verbal communication. If you were asked to identify just ten of the non-verbal messages, you may find it difficult, but we all know them and respond to them intuitively.

The key to using your intuition more effectively is to bring the unconscious data it supplies to a place where your conscious mind can interpret it. Intuition is always communicating to you. Occasionally, it may send a signal that turns out to be less than dangerous, but everything it communicates to you is meaningful.

Intuition might send any of several messengers to get your attention, and because they differ according to urgency, it is good to know the various messages.

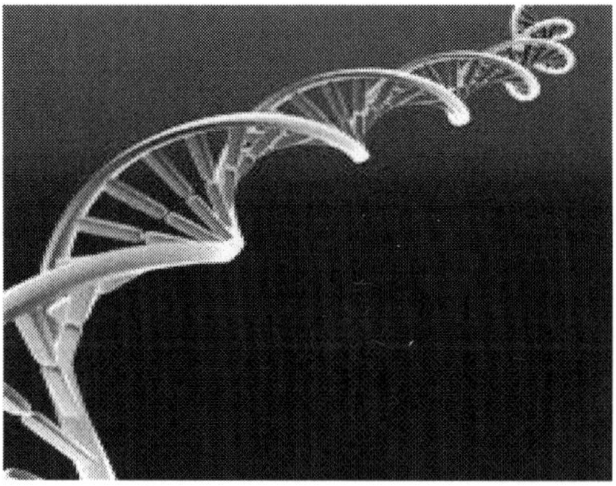

Messages of Intuition:

Synchronicity: This is the message all of us get. It the connectedness we all have and write off as airy-fairy. The best example of this is a phone call. All of us have been thinking about that particular someone and the phone rings and it's *them.* This happens to all of us, in many ways, every day.

"If there is anything intuition demonstrates, it's the interconnectedness of everything."

-Carl Jung, Synchronicity

- **Nagging Feelings:** When we experience nagging feelings about someone or something, it is our unconscious awareness telling us to wait and question what is going on.
- **Hunches:** A hunch is a feeling that a particular event or situation will go a certain way.
- **Gut Feeling:** A term many of us like to use in regard to predicting something that may or may not happen. For some of us a gut feeling is visceral, we can literally feel it.
- **Hesitation/Doubt:** When we hesitate and doubt we are stalling for more time and questioning the situation.
- **Suspicion:** For some, being suspicious is their internal radar that says, "something isn't right here."
- **Physical Changes:** Like other species, we too, change physically when exposed to internal and external intuitive messages. When the hair stands up on the back of your neck or when you get goose bumps, your body is telling you something.
- **Danger:** The intuitive messenger with the greatest urgency is DANGER. When you know with all of your being that you are in trouble or a situation is imminent is the intuitive message of danger.

Developing Intuition

Learning to read body language teaches us to be more sensitive to people's feelings and emotions, provide better customer service or care to those who rely on us, and increase our personal safety.

Developing your intuitive ability begins with paying attention to what's going on inside of you so that you can become aware of these inner signals and catch them when they are happening, or shortly afterward.

NOTE: The enemy of intuition is worry. When you play or replay negative situations, spending energy on things that have already happened or might happen soon, you don't have the mental space to acknowledge and act on signals your intuition is trying to send to you!

"He is most free from danger, who,
even when safe, is on his guard."

– Publilius Syrus, Latin writer of maxims, 1st century BC

Developing and using your intuition means you need to stop, look and listen occasionally to what your feelings, senses, perceptions and contexts of situations are telling you at that present moment. Listening to, trusting, and acting on your intuitive inner guidance is an art. And like any art or discipline, it requires an ongoing commitment. Challenge yourself to develop a deeper understanding of self-awareness.

"They that are on their guard and appear ready to receive
their adversaries are in much less danger of being attacked
than the supine, secure and negligent."

– Benjamin Franklin, one of the founding fathers of the USA

Chapter 6

Avoidance

"The best self-defense is to not be there when the attack takes place."

– David Fowler, Author of *Be Safe Not Sorry*.

Who commits violence? People do. The types of individuals who commit violence are categorized into four areas: stranger violence, guest/client violence, lateral violence and domestic violence. There are specific characteristics for all four types of individual violence listed below. After examining these characteristics, we will look at strategies to prevent, mitigate or eliminate your risk of violence from these individuals.

Stranger Violence Includes:

- Rape
- Robbery
- Assaults (verbal and physical)
- Bomb threats
- Gang violence

- Shootings, i.e. Active Shooters (that is, an armed person who uses deadly physical force on other persons and continues to do so while having unrestricted access to additional victims. The Columbine, Virginia Tech, and Tucson shootings were all instances of an Active Shooter).

Stranger violence also includes verbal threats, threatening behavior or physical assaults by an assailant who has no legitimate business or relationship to the workplace. This person may enter the workplace to commit a criminal act or robbery. In most states, violence by strangers accounts for most of the fatalities related to workplace violence.[7]

Guest/Client Violence

Guest, client or customer violence can involve verbal threats, threatening behavior or physical assaults by an assailant who either receives services from, or is under the custodial supervision of, the affected workplace or the victim. Guest/client violence is often the result of:

- Intoxication
- Mental illness
- Anger/aggression

[7] http://www.bls.gov/

- Stress/confusion
- Physical abnormalities
- Sexual aggression

Violence by guests, customers and clients accounts for the majority of non-fatal injuries related to workplace violence in many states.[8]

Lateral Violence

Perpetrated by co-workers, lateral violence includes:

- Bullying
- Intimidation
- Anger/aggression
- Sexual aggression

[8] http://www.bls.gov/

Lateral violence is often perpetrated by someone who was recently disciplined or discharged. It involves verbal threats, threatening behavior or physical assaults by an assailant who has some employment-related involvement with the workplace. Assailants could be a current or former employee, supervisor, manager, or contractor. Any workplace can be at risk of violence by a co-worker.

Recognizing early warning signs of Lateral Violence

No single sign alone should cause concern, but a combination of any of the following signs should be cause for concern and action:

- Direct or verbal threats of harm.
- Intimidation of others by words and or actions.
  Refusing to follow policies.
- Hypersensitivity or extreme suspiciousness.
  Extreme moral righteousness.

- Inability to take criticism regarding job performance. Holding a grudge, especially against a supervisor.
- Repeatedly verbalizing that something will happen to the other person against whom the individual has the grudge.
- Expression of extreme desperation over recent problems. Intentional disregard for the safety of others.
- Destruction of property.

An assailant who commits a threat or assault may be seeking revenge for a perceived unfair treatment. Lateral workplace violence fatalities can receive a lot of media attention, but only account for a small portion of all workplace violence related fatalities. Again, stranger violence accounts for most workplace violence fatalities.

Domestic Violence

Domestic violence can spill over into the workplace, and often involves:

- Significant others (spouse, lover, current or not)
- Family members (parents, siblings, etc.)
- Child custody issues
- Stalking
- Enemies
- Friends

Domestic violence in the workplace can involve verbal threats, threatening behavior or physical assaults by an assailant who has a personal relationship with someone in the workplace, but does not work in the same workplace.

The assailant's actions may be motivated by real or perceived difficulties in the relationship, or psychosocial factors specific to them.

More and more, domestic violence is spilling over into workplace violence. This is a terrifying trend, because you and your employees or co-workers could be in danger from someone you've never met, and may not even recognize if he/she came into your workplace.

According to study by the American Bar Association the FBI cites the following things as indicators of possible domestic violence or stalking: (**http://www.americanbar.org**), (**http://www.fbi.gov/statservices/publications/workplace-violence**)

The Following Observable Behavior May Suggest Possible Victimization

- Tardiness or unexplained absences
- Frequent and often unplanned use of leave time
- Anxiety
- Lack of concentration
- Change in job performance
- A tendency to remain isolated from coworkers or reluctance to participate in social events
- Discomfort when communicating with others
- Disruptive phone calls or e-mail
- Sudden or unexplained requests to be moved from public locations in the workplace, such as sales or reception areas
- Frequent financial problems indicating lack of access to money

- Unexplained bruises or injuries
- Noticeable change in use of makeup (to cover up injuries)
- Inappropriate clothes (e.g., sunglasses worn inside the building, turtleneck worn in the summer)
- Disruptive visits from current or former intimate partner
- Sudden changes of address or reluctance to divulge where she is staying
- Acting uncharacteristically moody, depressed, or distracted
- In the process of ending an intimate relationship, breakup seems to cause the employee undue anxiety
- Court appearances
- Being the victim of vandalism or threats

How Do You Protect Yourself From Domestic Violence In The Workplace?

1. Institute a culture of safety in your workplace—that means making people feel SAFE about reporting abuse. Often, a co-worker will report the things listed above. Encourage your employees to go to their supervisors and security personnel if they see anyone has been abused, if they've witnessed stalking behavior, or if they suspect a co-worker has been abused or is being stalked.

2. Remember, the abuse victim IS a victim. Be as subtle and considerate as possible when pulling this person aside to discuss what is going on in her/his home life. Explain to her/him that this DOES affect the workplace, and that, for the safety of this person at work, AND all co-workers, you are obligated to document the abuse. Again, please remember that you are dealing with a victim. Do not victimize her/him again.

3. Get the name, description, and, if at all possible, a photo of the abuser. Many abusers already have a criminal record, and mug shots are in the public domain.

4. Make sure ALL relevant personnel have this photo, and that they know what steps to take. If the victim has filed a restraining order, the front-line personnel need to DISCREETLY call 911.

5. If an employee comes to supervisors to report abuse, TAKE IT SERIOUSLY.

Predators

"People will object very much to seeing a predator killing its prey, and yet, in the news, will accept showing shots of people shooting one another."

– Sir David Attenborough, BBC Broadcaster and Naturalist

What is a predator?

1. An organism that lives by preying on other organisms.

2. One that victimizes, plunders, or destroys, especially for one's own gain.

A correlation can be made between predators in the wild and human predators in our society. A number of similarities are present with both animals and humans.

Predator-Prey and Adaptation

Adaptation is a basic phenomenon of biology, and also refers to a characteristic which is especially important to an organism's survival. Adaptive traits can be structural, behavioral, psychological and physiological.

Structural: We as humans secure our homes, cars, and workplaces with locks, solid doors/window and use security devices, etc., to keep us safe.

Behavioral: We have the ability to recognize threatening behaviors in others, as well as to behave in ways as to not cause unwanted attention or portray ourselves as easy targets.

Psychological: It all starts with having a mindset of awareness and vigilance.

Physiological: Is self-awareness of our physical ability to run, defend and take action if needed.

Predator and Prey

A predator may be larger than its prey, stronger and sometimes faster. Predators develop their senses and always seek opportune times to strike. They will camouflage themselves using their environment and behaviors. And a predator is not always specific in regards to its prey; often it will seek more than one prey or type of prey. Most crime and violence occur during evening and nighttime hours. But, be cautious, as some predators will choose daytime to prey upon their victims as well.

The predator doesn't want someone who will resist, so he or she will select prey that is older, weaker, or very young. The predator's prey can be either male or female. The predator knows that a person's presence sends a message about their confidence and ability; people who are unaware become easy prey for predators. People who stand out or call unnecessary attention to themselves are advertising themselves as prey. Those who are distracted can also be victimized. And isolation gives the predator protection from unwanted attention.

A typical police line-up is done with the suspects being lined up and the victim determining if any of the suspects in the line-up are the perpetrator of the crime. The reverse line-up is everyday people in everyday life, and the predator determines the prey he/she will select from that line-up. In a reverse line-up, predators are evaluating and selecting their prey from a pool of potential victims—us.

Don't Be Easy Prey: Don't be a victim. Don't be prey. Any of the mental states, or what is known as prey paradigms, listed below leave you vulnerable to observant predators. They'll know you're an easy target. Do not fall into these mental states—that's one of your best defenses for avoiding violence.

Un-Aware Unconsciously: An unconscious state of unawareness of a person's surroundings and the people they encounter. This unconscious state is not knowing that you don't know. But remember, ignorance is not a good defense.

Un-Prepared: A higher state of conscious awareness than being un-aware, but lacking in preparedness of potential situations. Have you ever said to yourself, "I'm just not that prepared for the day."

Un-Secured: Not using the precautionary security tools and equipment in a person's environments. Environmental components are in place to keep you safe. Not knowing where they are or how to use them is not a good defense.

Un-Aware Consciously: The most lacking in awareness is a dangerous state of denial—the "nothing can happen to me" mentality. It's when you just don't care and are consciously choosing to be unaware.

Un-Fortunate: Being in the wrong place at the wrong time. This paradigm mindset is the least likely event to happen; however, by increasing your awareness and your vigilance, you can lessen your chances of being in the wrong place at the wrong time.

Understanding the characteristics of individuals who commit violence, as well as what predators look for in their prey, increases your awareness and vigilance. And remember: if it doesn't feel right, it almost certainly isn't.

Hard Target vs. Easy Target

Predators will always choose the easier target. Easy targets are easily identifiable. Easy targets appear:

- Un-aware
- Have a non-confident presence
- Walk with a lackadaisical stride, with their eyes down, head down, and a slumped posture
- Use non-specific actions
- Have a timid or submissive presence

Predators will target easy prey and avoid prey that is harder or more of a risk for them. Having awareness and a presence that says "confidence" is the first step in avoiding a conflict with an assailant (predator).

Make yourself a hard target by:

Being aware: When it's obvious you are paying attention to what's around you, you are not an easy target.

Displaying a confident presence that deters predators. Do this by:

- Keeping your eyes up
- Keeping your head up
- Walking with erect posture
- Using a confident stride
- Moving purposefully.

All of these characteristics display a confident presence rather than a weak or easy target presence.

Assertive Presence: Assertiveness is the ability to exercise one's rights without denying the rights of others. We express our assertiveness with our body language, eye contact and voice. The opposite of assertive is to be inclined to timidity or lack of self-confidence. There are times when an assertive presence is needed in our interpersonal communications.

Defensive Presence: A defensive presence is only used when dealing with an aggressive individual(s). To avoid being seen as aggressive, stand with your body angled at forty-five degrees to another person. Most animals, when wanting to fight, will signal this approach by facing head on.

The Law of Cause and Effect: The Law of Cause and Effect basically states that for every movement of energy—such as in a natural happening, or a human thought that takes the form of an image, feeling, desire, belief, expectation or action—there is a corresponding effect. For this reason, the Law of Cause and Effect influences every aspect of your living experience. To determine why your living experience is of a certain quality, or why something has come into your life, you simply need to discover what causes preceded the effects. If and when you like the *effects* you are living with, then you keep the causes. If not, then you change the causes to create a different effect.

How does this help you avoid violence? Using your confident, assertive or defensive presence even when you do not feel like it can influence your thoughts and the situation. The same is true with our thoughts; when we have confident, assertive or defensive thoughts it can influence our bodies and the situation.

Developing Your Avoidance Ability

Of course, you have a lot more tools for avoidance than just a confident presence. Learning to use all the tools at your disposal will help you develop your avoidance ability.

Structural Avoidance: The use of any barrier, shield, device or protective layer around you and the security that they afford you. Most commonly these are your home, vehicle, and workplace., and the security that they afford you.

Behavioral Avoidance: The ability to recognize behaviors through reading body language is the oldest communication system. Trust in your ability to read others and know that you, too, are sending a message.

Psychological Avoidance: Mental awareness is having the ability to recognize dangers and make decisions, choices and responses that always keep you safe.

Physiological Avoidance: Having the ability to physically and defensively intervene in a situation. Your confident presence is also a huge physiological deterrent.

Environmental Avoidance: Using safety awareness for the different types of environments you are in. Similar to structural avoidance, but more broad in scope, as our environments are broad.

Intuitive Avoidance: When you are truly present in the moment, you can receive messages internally and externally. Trusting and acting on the messages will keep you aware and safe.

Chapter 7

Interpersonal Communications

"The meeting of two personalities is like the contact of two chemical substances: if there is any reaction, both are transformed."

- Carl Jung, Swiss Psychologist, 1875 – 1961

Interpersonal communications is a transactional process through which people share their ideas and feelings by simultaneously sending and receiving messages. It's a complex and dynamic process in which individuals interact with one another, usually face-to-face.

Messages may be exchanged verbally or non-verbally and may be sent intentionally or unintentionally.

Our ability to communicate with others can significantly reduce the potential for conflicts. Interpersonal communications skills involve the following:

Listening: Active listening is a structured way of listening and responding to others. It focuses attention on the other person.

Asserting: To state or express positively one's rights, beliefs or positions.

Influencing: Our power to affect people, actions and events.

Persuading: To succeed in causing a person to do, or consent to do, something.

Empathizing: To sense and understand someone else's feelings as if they were one's own.

Sensitivity: Being cognizant of emotional feelings (of self and others).

Diplomacy: Having tact and skill in dealing with people.

Develop Your Communications Skills

Communication skills involve much more than just speaking well. Albert Mehrabian was a pioneer researcher of body language. In his book, *Nonverbal Communication,* Mehrabian explained that 55% of communication is non-verbal, 38% is vocal (tone and inflection), and only 7% is verbal (words only). Our attitudes and emotions are continuously revealed on our faces—and most of us are completely un-aware of it. Most people form 60% to 80% of their initial opinion about a new person in just a few minutes.

To communicate effectively, you need to understand the 93% of communication that isn't verbal. Know what message you're sending—and accurately read the message being sent to you.

Facial Expressions: A smile is worn on every friendly face. Smiling and laughing are universally considered to be signals that show a person is happy. Smiling serves much the same purpose as it does with other primates: it tells another person you are non-threatening and asks them to accept you on a personal level.

Eye Contact: The three I's of eye communication are:

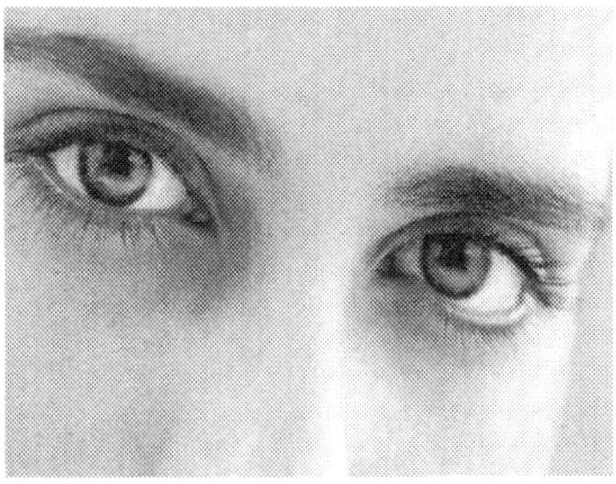

- Intimate
- Intimidating (a person will stare to intimidate or dominate another)
- Interested (the category of eye contact recommended for appropriate interpersonal communications).

Give the amount of eye contact that makes others feel comfortable and that you are interested in them. When talking, we maintain 40% to 60% eye contact, with an average of 80% when listening. To build good rapport with people, your eye contact should meet theirs about two-thirds of the time. (The exception to this is Japanese and some Asian and South American cultures where extended eye contact can be seen as aggressive or disrespectful.)

Body Language: Body language is an outward reflection of a person's emotional condition. Positive body language is linked to emotions, so changing your body language can change your attitude.

Postures: Stand up straight when talking and lean slightly forward when listening.

When a person has a nervous, negative or defensive attitude it is very likely they will fold their arms firmly on their chest, displaying that they feel threatened. Crossed arms on the chest are universally perceived as defensive or negative.

Gestures: Be expressive, but don't overdo it. Keep your fingers closed when you gesture, hands below chin level and avoid arm or feet crossing.

Nodding the head is almost universally used to indicate "yes" or agreement. Using multiple nods can be a persuasion tool. Research shows that people will talk three to four times more than usual when the listener nods their head in regular intervals.

Hands: The hands have been the most important tools in human evolution. There are more connections between the brain and the hands than any other body parts.

Throughout history, the open palm has been associated with truth, honesty, allegiance and submission. Hidden palms may give a person an intuitive feeling that the person they are communicating with is untruthful.

Universal hand signals are:

- Palms Up = Open
- Palms Out = Stop
- Palms Down = Authority

The "Right" Angle: When approaching individuals who are in the assault cycle (stressed, intoxicated, angry, combative), we should approach at a 45 degree angle versus approaching them head on. This type of approach reduces tension and is a safer approach.

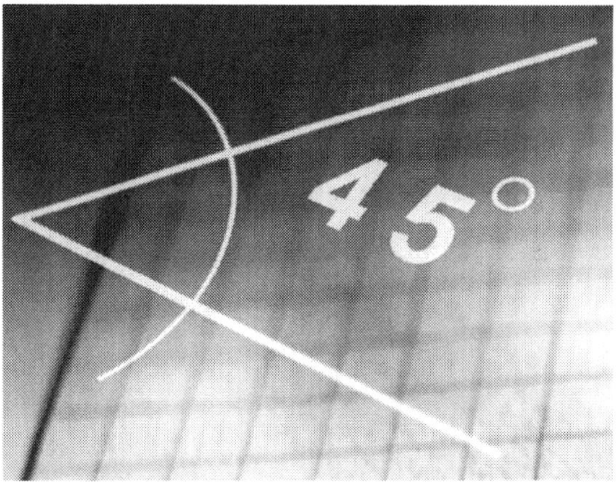

Cultural Differences: The biggest cultural differences exist mainly in relation to territorial space (distance), eye contact, touching, and insult gestures. The regions that have the greatest number of different gestures are Arab countries and parts of Asia and Japan.

Components of the Assault Cycle

The Assault Cycle is the predictable behavior that leads to violence. Understanding the Assault Cycle is crucial to knowing how to de-escalate and defuse a potentially dangerous situation to break the cycle before violence occurs or escalates.

Use caution when dealing with any of these behaviors, as they can be violence-predicting factors: stress, intoxication, anger and combative actions.

The following information will help you recognize the signs and symptoms of the behaviors as well as give you verbal and physical maneuvers to defuse and avoid violent behaviors.

Signs and Symptoms of Stress

- Change in facial expression—flushing
- Change in eye contact—darting, movement
- Change in speech—speeding up or slowing down
- Nervous nuances—twitching lips/face
- Acting distracted or confused
- Pacing and fidgeting
- Shallow breathing

Stress De-Escalation

Use these verbal and physical maneuvers and interventions to defuse and avoid violent behavior:

- Blade your body so the other person does not feel threatened.
- Use a slow, quiet and confident tone of voice.
- Control your behavior. If you get agitated, you will escalate the situation. Do not get sucked into the issue. Remember, I + R = O.
- Assess your body language—what signals are you sending? Avoid being rigid. Staying relaxed will encourage the other person to relax.
- Use names, the other individual's and yours. Introduce yourself and ask the individual their name. Personalizing a situation can reduce tension and establish a bond.
- Assess the area and space you're in, and stay at least 4' away and know your escape routes.
- Do not touch the individual. Touching a person may escalate the situation.
- Break eye contact to remain non-threatening and use your interested eye contact.
- Use attentive listening. Make sure the individual feels like he/she is being listened to.
- Do NOT make promises that you cannot keep.
- Clarify communications, and ask for specific responses. "You want ___, is that correct?" "What can I do to help you?" "Why are you upset?"
- Express your intention to help. "I am here to help"

- Redirect their thoughts and environment. We redirect thoughts by asking questions and we redirect environments by getting people to move to a new location or area.

Signs & Symptoms of Anger

Anger is a feeling related to one's perception of having been offended or wronged and a tendency to undo that wrongdoing by retaliation. Anger may lead to a person becoming combative if the person is unable to maintain control. All of us have been angry, and how we handle our anger and deal with another person's anger can determine the kind of outcome we want.

Signs and symptoms of anger include:

- Loud voice
- Challenging statements
- Foul language
- Verbal threats/veiled threats
- Physically acting out

- Pacing & tense
- Invading others' personal space
- Personal history of violence (knowledge of a person's background and history can be extremely important as it can be a pre-incident indicator of escalation to violence).
- Exaggerated movements
- Unwarranted claims
- Demanding unnecessary services, unnecessary attention, and entitlement
- Acting disgruntled
- Attempting to intimidate

Anger De-escalation

Remember to use all interventions for stressed individuals, and *use these* verbal and physical maneuvers to defuse and avoid violent behavior. Above all, control your own emotions and remember this QTIP: Quit Taking It Personally.

- Walk away if possible.
- Avoid arguing. Don't interrupt, and allow them to vent.
- Seek to agree and get them to say "yes."
- Use a collaborative approach—using "we" and "us"—gives a person a feeling of belonging.
- Display sincerity.
- Identify the problem. Ask them "Why are you angry?"
- Give options. Expressing feelings like the angry person has a choice may help them choose to calm down.

- Resist being defensive.
- Do not make threats.
- Ignore challenges.
- Set and enforce boundaries, but only ones you can enforce.
- Ask questions rather than give orders.

Intoxication

Intoxication (also known as drunkenness, inebriation, being high, under-the-influence, etc.) is a physiological state occurring when an individual has a high level of alcohol or drugs in their bloodstream. Intoxication can lower inhibitions and impair self-control, leading to violence. Anyone under the influence of alcohol or drugs—prescription or otherwise—falls into this category.

Signs of intoxication include:

- Slurred speech
- Impaired balance and/or poor coordination
- Flushed face

- Abnormal eyes--reddened, glossy, pupils dilated
- Up and down attitudes—euphoria, despair, etc.
- Reduced inhibition, erratic behavior
- Odors, on the person's breath or clothing
- Emotional response
- Argumentative
- Loud and obnoxious

Intoxication De-escalation: Remember to use stress and anger intervention techniques, as well as the verbal and physical maneuvers listed below, to defuse and avoid violent behavior with intoxicated individuals.

- Avoid intoxicated individuals when at all possible.
- Use caution and stay aware.
- Don't argue. Arguing with intoxicated individuals can escalate the situation.
- Be proactive in your responses.
- Seek to agree.
- Express your feelings. Expressing that you are frightened or scared of the person's behavior may de-escalate them.
- Assess the area for weapons, escape routes and maintain a proper distance from them.

Combative Aggression

Combative Aggression is behavior that is intended to cause pain or harm. Signs that an individual is about to become combative include:

- Changes in posture, such as dropping into a fighting stance.
- Telegraphing intentions; that is, you see an arm swing or get cocked before a punch is thrown.
- Looks at striking area. An assailant will almost always look at the area they intend to strike before the attack.
- Exaggerated movements.
- Changes in verbalization—either talking a lot more, or suddenly talking less.

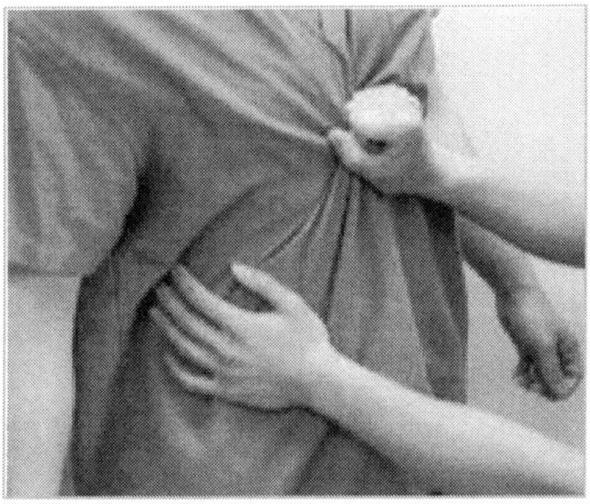

- Bracing effect, as though bracing to hit or be hit.
- Tightening of body and/or fists.
- Trying to distract you.

Strategies to Avoid Physical Harm with a Combative Person

- Escape immediately. That is the most important thing you can do. Once someone has reached the state of combative aggression, your number one priority is to get away.

- Defensive presence. Show you're ready to defend yourself, by blading your body and hands.
- Scream or yell as loudly as you can to attract attention.
- Yelling, "Stop!" can also arrest someone's attack.
- Use distractions to interrupt their focus and intent.
- Stay aware, and avoid tunnel vision.
- Watch to see what they are planning to do next.
- Get help. Alert others by motioning or verbalizing.
- Last resort is to use self-defensive techniques if your escape is impossible.

Submission

Just as important as knowing the signals of escalation is knowing the signals of submission. Submission is displayed through a significant cluster of body movements that are used to signal fear and readiness to submit. This is common in humans and animals, where fighting (that could terminally harm each animal) is avoided by displays of aggression or submission.

Signs & Symptoms of Submission

Body Positions: The body in fearful stances is generally closed and may also include additional aspects.

Self-Protection: Hunching inwards reduces the size of the body, limiting the potential of being hit and protecting vital areas; for example, hands covering crotch or chin pushed down to protect the neck.

In a natural setting, being small may also reduce the chance of being seen. Arms are held in. A crouching position may be taken, even slightly with knees slightly bent. This is approaching the curled-up regressive fetal position.

Lowering: Putting the body in a lower position shows the other person that you are not a physical threat. This can include hunching down, bowing, kneeling or even prostration. It is no surprise that these are typically used in formal greetings of a superior person. Even in sitting, a submissive person will choose a lower chair or slump in order to be lower than others are.

Motionlessness: By staying still, the chance of being seen is, in a natural setting, reduced (which is why many animals freeze when they are fearful). When exposed, it also reduces the chance of accidentally sending signals which may be interpreted as being aggressive. It also signals submission, in that you are ready to be struck and will not fight back.

Head Down: Turning the chin and head down protects the vulnerable neck from attack. It also avoids looking the other person in the face (staring is a sign of aggression).

Eyes Down: Widening the eyes makes you look more like a baby and hence signals your vulnerability. Looking attentively at the other person shows that you are hanging on to their every word.

Mouth (Smile): Submissive people smile more at dominant people, but they often smile with the mouth but not with the eyes.

Submissive Gestures: There are many gestures that have the primary intent of showing submission and that there is no intent to harm the other person. Hands out and palms up shows that no weapons are held and is a common pleading gesture. Other gestures and actions that indicate tension may indicate the state of fear. This includes hair tugging, face touching and jerky movement. There may also be signs such as whiteness of the face and sweating.

Small Gestures: When the submissive person must move, then small gestures are often made. These may be slow to avoid alarming the other person, although tension may make them jerky.

Submissive Verbalization: Common verbalization will be, "I'm sorry," "I shouldn't have...," "I didn't mean to," "I apologize," "what can I do?" "You're right; I'm wrong," etc.

Dealing with people who are stressed, angry, intoxicated or combative can be a frightening experience. For some it is part of their daily experience at their workplace. No matter what you do, your interpersonal communications can help you recognize and diffuse a potentially violent situation.

Some general things to keep in mind when using your interpersonal communication skills:

- Be clear and concise when speaking.
- Avoid using slang and jargon when speaking to people. It helps avoid confusion, misdirection, complaints and poor interpersonal relations.
- Play the part of the scene you are currently in. "All the world is indeed a stage and we are merely players." As the stage changes, play the appropriate part to keep yourself safe.
- The Golden Rule is the rule of treating others as you would like to be treated. Treating and speaking to people with respect is a universally accepted standard of treating people. "Do unto others as you would have them do unto you."
- The Platinum Rule teaches us to treat others the way *they* want to be treated.
- Use common courtesies *consistently* and *repeatedly* with all people, all the time.

    -Please.

    -Thank you.

    -Yes, please.

    -My pleasure.

    -You're welcome.

    - I am sorry to disturb you, but I need to speak with you a moment.

- People watch and pay attention. Watch and learn as you view the stage that others are on. Pay attention to what works and doesn't work for you and other people.

- Learn from your experiences and the experiences of others. Experience is a great teacher.

Knowledge and training are the the key to understanding and avoiding situations that are threatening and unsafe. When faced with a situation that is unavoidable and threatening, we may need to physically intervene to defend ourselves or another person.

Chapter Eight

Defense of Self and Others

"The best and safest thing is to keep a balance in your life, acknowledge the great powers around us and in us. If you can do that, and live that way, you are really a wise man."

– Euripides, Greek dramatist (484-406 B.C.)

Self-defense is the right to use reasonable force to protect one's self or members of one's staff/family from bodily harm from the attack of an aggressor if you have reason to believe that you or they are in danger. Self-defense must always be your last resort. When it is used, the force used must be considered "reasonable"; i.e., striking someone who yells an obscenity at you is not considered "reasonable force."

The best self-defense is to *avoid the situation and get away*. If avoidance and escape are not possible, a reasonable defense would be lawful as a last resort. You have the right to defend yourself; however, any use of self-defense must follow any agency policy and procedure, as well as follow state and federal law.

The following information will provide a general understanding of what self-defense and use-of-force are, and how you can legally protect yourself against assault and liability risk associated with any type of self-defense or force.

Disclaimer

This chapter will give you a basic understanding of self-defense, assault, reasonable force and basic legal definitions of force. Personal Safety Training Inc. makes no legal declaration, representation or claim as to what force should be used or not used during a self-defense or assault incident or situation. Each individual must take into consideration their ability, agency policies and procedures, and laws in the state and country in which they reside.

Types of Assault

Physical Assault: The attempt to cause injury, coupled with the present ability to cause injury.

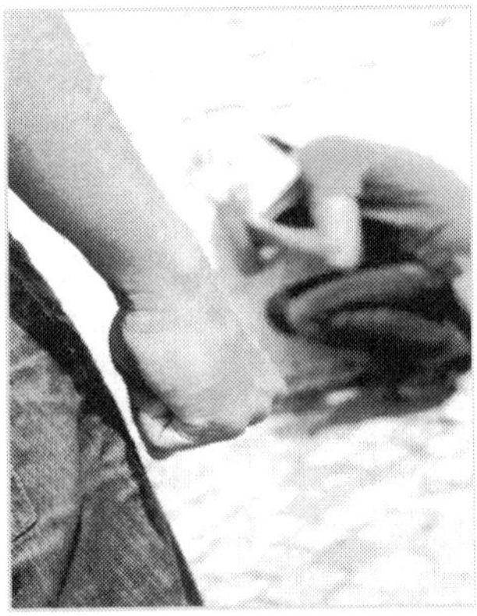

Non-Physical Assault: Physical contact is not required to constitute an assault. In all states, threats are a separate crime. A verbal threat of physical harm is one with the intent to intimidate or scare, with the result altering any part of a person's normal life due to the threat.

To constitute an illegal threat, the following must be true:

- The threat must be serious with the threat of definite injury.
- The threat must be immediate, and can be carried out in the immediate or near future.
- The threat must be credible; that is, the victim believes the threat and acts upon that belief.

Domestic Assault: Can involve battery that occurs between two parties who are related by some degree (family or intimate relationships).

Battery Assault: Battery is a criminal offense whereby one party makes physical contact with another party with the intention to harm them. In order to constitute battery, an offense must be intentional and must be committed to inflict injury on another.

Sexual Battery: Any non-consensual physical contact that is sexual in nature.

Lawful Use of Defense

In order to be lawful in your defense of yourself and others, you must have a basic understanding of some legal definitions and how they apply to self-defense and our legal system.

Reasonable Force: The degree of force which is not excessive and is appropriate in protecting one's self or one's property. When such force is used, a person is justified and is not criminally liable, nor is he liable in tort. (A tort is an act that damages someone in some way, and for which the injured person may sue the wrongdoer for damages.)

Reasonable Belief: The facts or circumstances that an individual knows, or should know, are such as to cause an ordinary and prudent person to act or think in a similar way under similar circumstances.

Deadly Force: Force that is likely, or intended, to cause death or great bodily harm. Deadly force may be reasonable or unreasonable, depending on the circumstances

Excessive Force: That amount of force which is beyond the need and circumstances of the particular event, or which is not justified in the light of all the circumstances, as in the case of deadly force to protect property as contrasted with protecting life.

Weapons: "Dangerous weapons" include any firearm, whether loaded or unloaded, or device designed as a weapon and capable of producing death or great bodily harm. A "deadly weapon" is a device or instrument which, in the manner it is used or intended to be used, is calculated or likely to produce death or great bodily harm.

The Civilian Levels of Defense chart on the following page is designed to give you an understanding of how to use defense in a lawful manner.

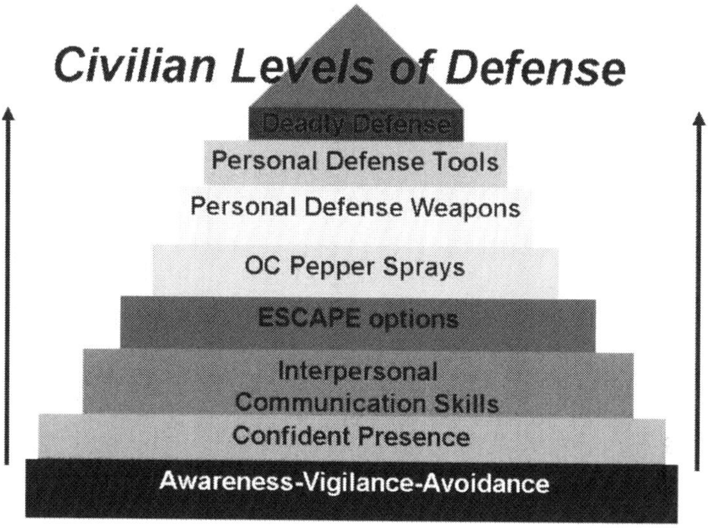

Level 1: Be aware, use your vigilance and avoid conflicts. This is the base of the chart, and the most important aspect of self-defense.

Level 2: Don't be an easy target. Your confident presence can be a major deterrent against violent offenders/predators. Using confident postures, facial expressions and eye communication show that you are not an easy target.

Level 3: Use your interpersonal communications skills when faced with people who are stressed, angry, intoxicated or combative;, your best initial defense is your ability to communicate.

Level 4: Know your escape options. When faced with a situation that is escalating and dangerous, if possible we should escape to a safe location and alert others. (See Chapter 9 for more on Escape.)

Level 5: OC Pepper Spray is a non-lethal force option which can distract the violent offender/predator, giving you time to escape or defend.

Level 6: Personal Defensive Weapons include unarmed defenses such as, our bodies, hands, feet and self-defense escape techniques.

Level 7: Personal Defense Tools include any non-deadly items which we can use in our hands to defend ourselves. Examples: key chains, umbrellas, flashlights, rolled up newspaper, etc.

Level 8: Deadly Defense is defense against what you believe to be a dangerous/deadly weapons/assault upon you.

Special Note:
Every person must take into consideration their moral, legal, and ethical beliefs and rights and understandings when using any type of force to defend themselves or others. Personal Safety Training Inc. makes no legal declaration, representation or claim as to what force should be used or not used during a self-defense/assault incident or situation. Each individual must take into consideration their ability, agency policies and procedures and laws in their state and/or country.

Post Incident Response

It's vital for all employers to have a Post-Incident Response protocol. The following points are guidelines for the proper and most efficient response to a violent incident.

Triage (Medical/Hazmat): Triage is the process of determining the priority of patients/victims treatments based on the severity of their condition. Initial first-aid treatment and protocols for hazardous materials/clean-up should be handled immediately.

Consider All Involved: Staff, guests, visitors or anyone who was witness to the incident should be treated accordingly for medical and stress debriefing.

Provide for Incident Debriefing: Debriefing allows those involved with the incident to process the event and reflect on its impact. Depending on the situation, a thorough debriefing may need to take place. Even those not specifically involved in an incident may suffer emotional and psychological trauma.

Critical Incident Stress Debriefing (CISD) is a specific technique designed to assist others in dealing with physical or psychological symptoms that are generally associated with critical incident trauma exposure. Research on the effectiveness of critical incident debriefing techniques has demonstrated that individuals who are provided critical stress debriefing within a 24- to 72-hour window after the critical incident and experience have less short-term and long-term crisis reactions and psychological trauma. (See Chapter 9 for more detail on CISD).

Employee Assistance Programs (EAP) EAPs are intended to help employees deal with work/personal problems that might adversely impact their work performance, health, and well-being. EAPs generally include assessment, short-term counseling and referral services for employees and their household members. Employee benefit programs offered by many employers, typically in conjunction with a health insurance plans, provide for payment for EAPs. (See Chapter 9 for more detail on EAPs).

Document incident to include any follow-up investigations: Post incident documentation is absolutely critical for reducing liability risk, preventing reoccurrences and follow-up investigations. (See below for more detail.)

Initiate corrective actions to prevent reoccurrences:
Preventing similar future incidents, involves taking proactive corrective actions. Agency management, supervision, risk management,

employee safety committees, environment of care committees, etc. should initiate, track and follow up on corrective actions.

Post Incident Documentation

WWWWWH

The first rule in post incident documentation is the "who, what, where, when, why and how" rule of reporting. After writing an incident narrative, double-check to see if you have included the first rule of reporting.

Witnesses

Make sure to include anyone who was a witness to the incident. Staff, visitors, guests and support services (police, fire, EMS, etc.) can be valuable witnesses should an incident be litigated.

Narrative Characteristics

A proper narrative should describe in details the characteristics of the violent offender/predator.

Before, During and After

A thorough incident report will describe what happened before, during and after the incident. Details matter!

1st Person vs. 3rd Person

The account of an incident can be described in first person or third person. This can be specific to your agency protocols or the preference of the person documenting the incident.

Post Follow-Up (track and trend)

Most agencies use electronic documentation, which allows for easy retrieval, tracking and trending. Using technology assists agencies to follow up and initiate proactive corrections.

Follow Standard Operating Procedures

Whether it is handwriting incident reports or electronic documentation and charting, staff should consistently and thoroughly document all incidents relating to violence in the workplace.

Chapter 9

Stress Management

"If you are distressed by anything external, the pain is not due to the thing itself, but to your estimate of it; and this you have the power to revoke at any moment."

– Marcus Aurelius Antoninus (121 AD - 180 AD)

Stress is physical, emotional or mental strain or tension brought on by internal and external factors.

In 1975, Hans Selye, a doctor of medicine and chemistry, published a model that divides stress into distress and eustress. Persistent stress that is not resolved by a coping mechanism or adaptation is deemed distress. Distress may lead to anxiety, withdrawal, and depression. Stress that enhances functions (physical or mental, such as through strength training or challenging work) is considered eustress.

The difference between eustress and distress is the result of the stress determined by a person's experience (real or imagined), their expectations, and their resources to cope with the stress.

"Adopting the right attitude can convert a negative stress into a positive one."

– Dr. Hans Selye

FEAR

Fear is a distressing emotion aroused by a perceived threat. It is a basic survival mechanism that occurs in response to a specific stimulus, such as pain or the threat of danger. Some psychologists suggest that fear belongs to a small set of basic or innate emotions. This set also includes such emotions as joy, sadness, and anger. Fear should be distinguished from the related emotional state of anxiety, which typically occurs without any external threat.

Additionally, fear is related to the specific behaviors of escape and avoidance, whereas stress is the result of threats that are perceived to be uncontrollable or unavoidable. Worth noting is that fear almost always relates to future events, such as worsening of a situation, or continuation of a situation that is unacceptable. Fear could also be an instant reaction to something presently happening.

"Fight-Flight-Freeze"

You've heard of fight-or-flight, which is a reaction to a threat with a general discharge of the sympathetic nervous system, priming the organism for fighting or fleeing. If completely overwhelmed, a person may freeze.

The fight-flight-freeze response is a basic, primal, physiological urge to defend or to flee in times of danger. When faced with a situation that is frightening, your perception of it stimulates the part of the brain called the hypothalamus. The hypothalamus emits a hormone that stimulates the pituitary gland to release substances that excite the adrenal gland to release adrenalin (epinephrine) and cortisone. Adrenalin stimulates the heart to beat faster and the vessels carrying blood to the muscles to open. The vessels that run the digestive and eliminative organs constrict. Blood pressure goes up, and more blood is being pumped, but many vessels constrict to slow the blood flow. Breath becomes faster and shallower, or you hold your breath. Blood shunts systematically from the vegetative organs to the muscles preparing you to fight or take flight.

Putting the Brakes on the Fight-Flight-Freeze response
Conscious Controlled Breathing and Conscious Positive Thinking are considered the best stress management techniques for immediate stressors (fight-flight) and ongoing stressors of life.

"Life is in the breath. He who half breathes, half lives."
- Ancient proverb

Conscious Controlled Breathing is a very useful tactic in lowering our blood pressure. Studies have shown that during the process of slow, deep breathing, endorphins are released causing a feeling of general well-being and relaxation. Endorphins apply a brake to the hypothalamic fight-flight response in a situation of imminent danger. Try this: inhale slowly, about two-thirds of your lung capacity. Breathe in for a count of four seconds; breathe out slowly to a count of eight seconds. Notice you immediately feel calmer.

Conscious Positive Thinking and calm mental preparation were recognized to be highly valuable to the Samurai of feudal Japan. In fact, the Samurai spent as much time in mental training as they did preparing their bodies for battle. Samurai employed two techniques to prepare the mind to be tranquil, fearless, and energetic in combat:

breath control and meditation. The Samurai knew that a warrior filled with fear (negative thoughts) is doomed. Fear inhibits the ability to think quickly or to act fully.

Caution: All strategies and methods for managing your stress should take into consideration your physical and mental health. Consult your physician prior to any changes in your behavior.

Strategies for Managing Your Stress Before an Incident of Workplace Violence

Healthy Eating

Proper nutrition and healthy eating habits can help you get through stressful times. Eating well will increase your physical, mental, and emotional stamina. Fueling yourself with food high in nutrients can boost your immune system, help you maintain a healthy weight and help you feel better about yourself.

Regular Exercise

Frequent exercise is one of the best physical stress-reduction techniques. Exercise not only improves your health and reduces stress, it also relaxes tense muscles and helps you to sleep better. Most importantly, there is evidence that suggests that physically fit people have less severe physiological responses when under stress than those who are not.

Proper Hydration

Stress can lead to dehydration. Dehydration affects thinking, causes headaches, nausea, constipation and irritability. Water is essential to your wellbeing.

Time Management

Planning your day can help you accomplish more and feel more in control of your life. Write a to-do list, putting the most important tasks at the top. Keep a schedule of your daily activities to minimize conflicts and last-minute rushes. Prioritize your tasks and say no to nonessential tasks.

Positive Thoughts

Negative thoughts and energy can affect you in many ways and cause you additional stress. Because of this, developing more positive thoughts is an important way to reduce stress in your life. You can help yourself maintain and increase positive thoughts by listening to uplifting music, reading inspirational books, spending time with positive people, and using positive affirmations.

Touch Therapy

Touch is the first sense to develop in humans. It is essential to our health and wellbeing. Babies have been known to fail to thrive and even die without an adequate amount of physical contact. Adults, as well, can become depressed and ill if they are isolated from this most basic of human needs.

Support System

It doesn't take a scientific study to show that surrounding yourself with supportive family, friends and co-workers can have a positive effect on your mental well-being. A strong social support network can be critical to help you through the stress of tough times, whether you've had a bad day at work, or a year filled with loss or chronic illness.

Recreation

Recreational activities are experiences in which you actively participate in an organized activity, generally with others, to have fun and enjoy life. They include participation in sports, arts and crafts, games, dancing, or any activity that takes involvement and participation.

Nature

Use nature to reduce stress. Go outside, hike in the woods, walk on the beach, anything that puts you in contact with the natural world. It is difficult to feel stressed when you are surrounded by nature's abundance of vitality and wonder.

Sacred Space

Sacred space is defined as any place where you're temporarily sealed off from the world. This can be a room, a special chair, even an activity, or just a state of mind. But the idea is that when you're in sacred space, whatever you're doing becomes a meditation or a peaceful state for your mind and body. Creating and maintaining your sacred space is a great way to reduce stress.

Post-Incident Stress Debriefing

The methods described above help manage your stress before an incident occurs. The methods described below will help you manage stress *after* an incident of workplace violence.

Always debrief. Staff should debrief after every workplace violence incident, regardless of the severity. Oftentimes a brief discussion of the events and outcome is enough. Other times, a more intensive debriefing is needed. The goal of debriefing is to reduce the chances of Post-Traumatic Stress Disorder, or PTSD.

Talk to co-workers. Almost all workers have experienced or witnessed some type of workplace violence incident. Your co-workers can be a great source to vent your concerns about your post feelings.

Acknowledge humanness. As humans we are susceptible to the frailties of human nature. This acknowledgement creates an awareness that it is okay to seek and ask for help.

Be aware of post-event feelings. Having the knowledge and awareness that you may experience strong feelings from an event can give you the confidence to seek help and discuss feelings with others.

Take advantage of your Employee Assistance Program (EAP). Agencies realize that post feelings may remain for longer periods of time after an incident. Employee Assistance Programs can benefit employees and help them deal with post incident stress or other work/personal problems. EAPs are intended to help employees deal with issues/problems that might adversely affect their work performance, health, and well-being. EAPs generally include assessment, short-term counseling and referral services for employees and their household members.

Know the signs and symptoms of Post-Traumatic Stress Disorder (PTSD). A psychological reaction occurring after experiencing a highly stressing event (such as wartime combat, physical violence, or a natural disaster), PTSD is usually characterized by depression, anxiety, flashbacks, recurrent nightmares, and avoidance of reminders of the event.

Take the time to follow-up with other staff. As human beings, we often focus on the needs of others and not ourselves. Take the time to discuss workplace incidents, your feelings about the incidents, and how incidents in the workplace could improve.

Find some Critical Incident Stress Debriefing (CISD). Debriefing is a specific technique designed to assist people in dealing with the physical or psychological symptoms that are generally associated with trauma exposure. Debriefing allows those involved with the incident to process the event and reflect on its impact. Individuals who are exposed to an assault situation (as a witness or a victim) should consider some level of critical incident debriefing or counseling.

The final extent of any traumatic situation may never be known or realistically estimated in terms of trauma, loss and grief. In the aftermath of any critical incident, psychological reactions are quite common and are fairly predictable. CISD can be a valuable tool following a traumatic event.

Research on the effectiveness of critical incident debriefing techniques has demonstrated that individuals who are provided CISD within a 24- to 72-hour period after the critical incident experience less short-term and long-term crisis reactions, psychological trauma, and PTSD.

Chapter 10

Time and Distance

The concept of time or distance illustrates that having time or distance can give us distance or time from a violent person, place, event or thing. What we do with our time can be the most precious investment we ever make. Imagine that you have the ability to use time and distance to your advantage. And remember:

Time and Distance = Safety

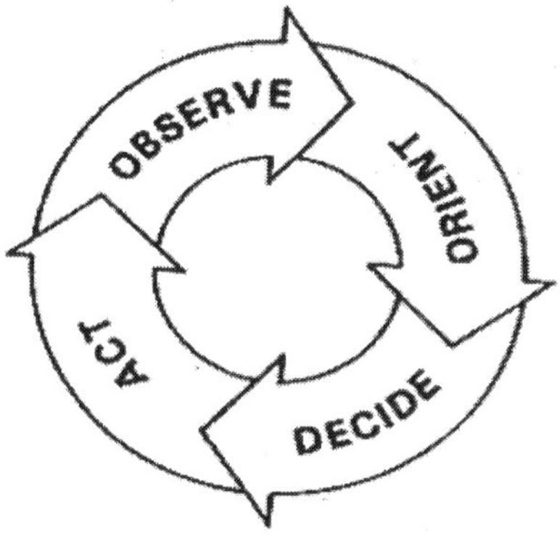

Reaction Time (OODA Loop)

Air Force Colonel John Boyd coined the term "OODA Loop" to describe a form of reaction time and decision-making. OODA stands for: observe-orient-decide-act.

Boyd's key concept is that the decision cycle is the process by which an individual reacts to an event. Accordingly, the key to victory is to be able to create situations wherein one can make appropriate decisions more quickly than one's opponent. This was originally a theory of achieving success in air-to-air combat.

Time is the dominant parameter in the OODA Loop. The individual who goes through the OODA Loop in the shortest time prevails, because his opponent is caught responding to situations that have already changed.

Observation: The collection of relevant data through your senses.

Orientation: The analysis of observed data to form your current mental perspective of what is happening.

Decision: Determining a course of action based on one's current mental perspective.

Action: The physical acting-out of your decisions.

Weapons and Time/Distance

Being faced with a weapon is terrifying. Know what to do ahead of time, and use the OODA Loop to your advantage.

Unarmed Attacks

You need a distance of at least four to six feet, which will give you time to escape from an attack. Variables that can affect this are environment and your physical ability.

Clubs and Sticks

When encountering an individual with a club, stick, or any type of impact weapon, the best defense is to create the biggest distance between you and them as you can. Studies have shown that individuals with weapons can cover a distance of twenty-one feet in approximately 1.5 seconds.

Knives/Edged or Sharpened Weapons

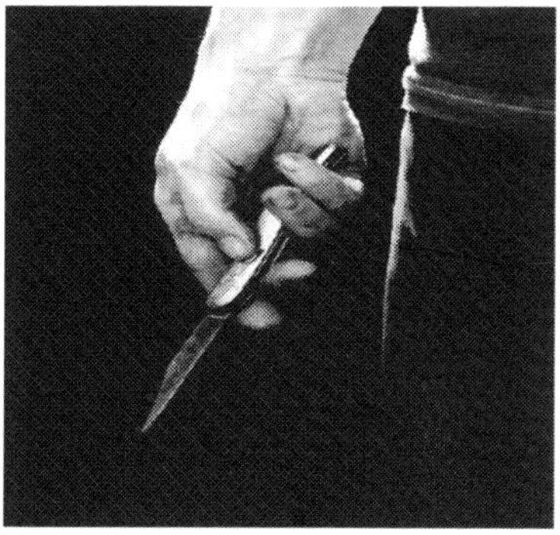

Twenty-one feet is the minimum distance you need from a person with any type of edged weapon. Your use of defense will need to escalate to defend yourself against any type of weapon being used against you. Again, your best defense is always to escape when possible.

Thrown Objects

Like the above weapons, a thrown object (chair, table, computer, etc.) can seriously injure an individual. Creating as much distance as possible between you and the aggressor is recommended.

Guns

In an active shooter situation, the best defense is to seek cover. Examples of cover: locations such as a safe room, behind a large barrier that is impenetrable, away from the area in stairwells, elevators, etc. Without the ability to seek cover, your best defense is to ESCAPE. Move! Run zig-zag, jump, and keep moving away until you are in a covered position. It is very difficult for a person to hit a moving target. Experienced law enforcement officers/trainers will tell you that a moving target is far harder to hit that a fixed target. Couple that with creating distance and you have a better chance at surviving. (More on the "active shooter" in Chapter 12.)

Dangerous Weapons in YOUR workplace

Learn the best way to protect from, and respond to, any use of a regular item that suddenly becomes a weapon.

Pens

Carry your pens so that they cannot be grabbed off of your person and used against you. A pen can easily impale the human body. Pens are a common tool that we all use. Increase your awareness by knowing that they can also harm you when in the hands of an out-of-control, combative individual.

Chairs

Escape immediately if a person has grabbed a chair and is preparing to throw it at you.

Glass/Beverages

Glass and other hard items that hold beverages and food can be thrown or used to strike at you. The contents in these can also be used to assault you—hot beverages such as coffee/tea.

Name Badges/Lanyards

Use caution with anything that is around your neck.

Items that can be moved or picked up.

Anything that can be picked up can be used as a weapon—staplers, heavy binders, small copiers, etc.

Edged Weapons: scissors, utensils, letter openers, etc.
Be cautious and aware that edged weapons are almost everywhere in the workplace environment. Kitchen utensils and office items are in most work environments and may pose a threat in the hands of an aggressor.

The Art of Distraction is a process by which you can buy valuable time to escape or defend. Distractions affect the senses, which take time for the mind to process the new information. They mainly affect a person's sight and sense of hearing; however, psychological distractions, such as asking a person something completely out of the ordinary can cause a mental delay as well.

Distractions have been used since ancient times and are a valuable advantage you should always use.

Sounds: Using a loud scream or yell can cause a momentary delay.

Movements: Using your hands, eyes, and body can distract and cause a momentary delay.

Psychological: Asking a person something completely out of the ordinary can cause them to have a mental delay. (i.e., "What color socks are you wearing?")

Lights: Flashlights, the sun, emergency lights, etc., can cause a delay.

Learning to use time and distance can keep you safe, unhurt and alive in instances of workplace violence.

Chapter 11

Escape Planning

"He who fails to plan, plans to fail."

-Proverb

"Planning is bringing the future into the present so that you can do something about it now."

– Alan Lakein, author of
How to Get Control of Your Time and Your Life

Developing escape plans for your various environments prepares you for the unfortunate event that you may need to escape from in a dangerous situation. This preparation is not intended to make you scared or paranoid, but to prepare you for the unexpected.

The first thing is to learn where all the exits are, in all environments you're in. It's a habit that could save your life. But not only are physical escapes needed, so are quick verbal responses that detach you from potential situations that can be negative, threatening and potentially dangerous or embarrassing.

Prepare for the worst, hope for the best,
and expect some surprises along the way."

- David Fowler, author and creator of AVADE® Training

Own the Door

The concept of "own the door" is to not allow others between you and the door (your escape route) when dealing with individuals who are in crisis; i.e. angry, highly stressed, recently terminated, intoxicated or combative. Position yourself so that you can escape if the situation becomes uncomfortable or dangerous. The environmental design of a facility can be limiting, but your awareness of your escape routes is the most important. With multiple individuals (visitors/guests/family members) in a room, politely ask them to all move to the furthest side of the room away from the doorway.

The best defense is to not be there when the attack takes place (avoidance), but if your escape route is compromised your last resort may be to defend yourself from an imminent attack. Always position yourself with an escape route in mind.

Dominant Hand / Proper Positioning

If a person becomes combative, they will more than likely strike you with their dominant hand. Positioning yourself on their dominant side makes it more difficult for them to strike at you. When dealing with at-risk individuals, position yourself on the dominant side of them.

Proper Positioning

You are always safer when you're at a 45-degree angle to a person who is upset. When standing, approaching, providing service to upset individuals and escorting individuals, use a 45-degree angle. This position is less threatening than facing them face to face, is a de-escalation technique and is the safest position for you to be in.

- Safe = 45 degrees in front of individual
- Safest = 45 degrees behind individual
- Unsafe = directly in front of an individual

Distance from the individual is also a major component of proper positioning.

"**Spatial empathy"** is an informal term used to describe the awareness of an individual to the proximity, activities and comfort of people around them. Having spatial empathy means that you are aware of your personal zones and the personal zones of other people around you. Having awareness that being in other people's personal zones may make them uncomfortable allows you to better serve and be safer.

Proper Escort is used for individuals in crisis. The ABCs of proper escort are:

- Have the individual walk in front of you.
- Maintain a 45-degree angle to them with proper distance.
- Use your verbal and non-verbal skills to direct them where you want them to go.
- Avoid pointing and maintain your awareness.

Relationship Escape Plans refers to determining your escape route ahead of time in relation to the people you are around or come in contact with.

Developing Escape Plans

When it comes to developing escape plans, keep in mind the following:

Commitment: You must look at all your environments and preplan your escape routes. Saying you'll do it tomorrow turns into someday, which turns into no follow-through.

Involvement: Management should ensure that all staff know the plan. When discussing plans with staff, management should be serious and matter-of-fact. The leadership role when advising departmental staff members should be confident and free of emotional fear.

Practice: Just like your kids do fire drills at school, you should physically and mentally run through the events of your escape. Have a schedule and practice routinely.

"What if?" Game: The "What if?" Game means playing mental scenarios of situations that may arise and force us to take action. The best emergency responders and police officers play the "What if?" Game regularly.

Changes: Realize now that things are going to change. You are going to change and so are most things in life. With this said, doesn't it make sense to update your escape plans as your life changes?

Environments: Environmental Awareness means that you have an understanding of the different types of vulnerabilities and resilience that your surroundings have or don't have.

Relationships: Escape planning always involves more than its physical nature. Successful personal safety involves communication skills that enable us to escape situations involving interpersonal relationships. A sharp awareness is keen to the sharp tongue.

Chapter 12

Environmental Factors

"You are a product of your environment. So choose the environment that will best develop you toward your objective. Analyze your life in terms of its environment. Are the things around you helping you toward success—or are they holding you back?"

- W. Clement Stone, Successful American Entrepreneur and Best-Selling Author (1902-2002)

Environments are a combination of external physical conditions that affect and influence the growth, development, and survival of organisms. Workers move through many environments, even if they only work in one department. From parking lots, to cafeterias, corridors and lobbies, environments are unique in their associated risks.

Environmental safety measures are put in place in workplaces to assist staff in protecting their environments, limiting access to their environments, and alerting others to assist them.

The following environmental safety measures are in place in multiple areas of the workplace environment:

Safety Mirrors

You use mirrors every day in your vehicle to keep yourself safe and aware of what's around you. If available, use the safety mirrors in your environment to alert you of obstacles, threats, and so that you can yield to guests and visitors.

Lighting

"Criminals don't like lights." It's an age-old axiom. Good lighting can discourage prowling or loitering. Always park and walk in areas with adequate lighting: entryways, pathways and stairwells.

Cameras – CCTV

Closed circuit television allows you to see what is happening in different areas of your department, or the entire workplace. It also helps the security/surveillance department to monitor from a remote location. CCTV is great deterrent against criminals; however, if no one is watching at the moment an incident happens no responders will be alerted. CCTV then becomes a tool for retrieving video after the fact.

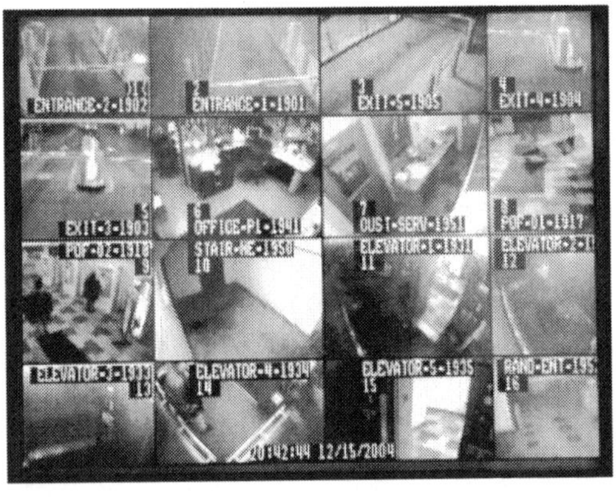

Some panic alarm systems are connected to a central security dispatch center. When activated, the camera in that immediate area pops up on their monitor. But not all security systems have this in place.

Panic Alarms

A panic or monitored alarm sends a signal to a remote location alerting them (usually security) to a breach in your security. These devices are mainly silent and are mounted in inconspicuous areas (under desk tops etc.). Proper training and education on using alarms is essential to their use. Alarms should be regularly tested for their efficiency.

Many key chains/fobs have a remote panic button that activates an audible alarm in the vehicle. This can be beneficial in parking lots and residences. Criminals are distracted by loud noises that alert and draw attention.

Private Places: Stairwells & Elevators, Restrooms, etc.

Avoid using isolated, unused stairways in your environment. When using elevators, stand near the control panel by the door so you can easily press the alarm button in an emergency.

If a suspicious-looking person follows you into an elevator, step out of the elevator immediately. If you see a suspicious-looking person inside an elevator you are about to enter, do not get in. If you are in an elevator and another person makes you feel uncomfortable, get off as soon as possible. Trust your instincts! Restrooms can isolate a person and compromise their escape route. If private restrooms are unavailable, lock doors, check stalls before entering, lock stall doors, and trust your instincts.

Access Controls (door locks)

Access controls are designed to keep people out of specific areas. Memorize codes, be aware of who is around you when entering a locked area, and do not give codes or access to anyone who is unauthorized to be in the particular area. Be cautious of "piggy backing"—when someone enters an accessed area right after an authorized person has entered, following them in without approved access. Security systems are only as good as the people using them. Learn how to use your security system properly.

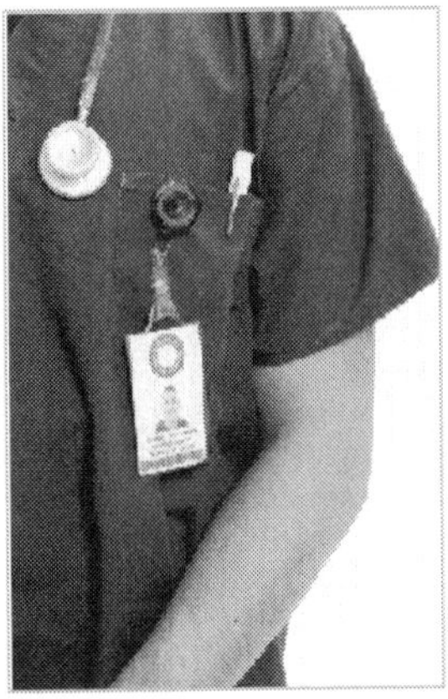

Staff Identification

These days, most employees are required to wear a visible ID with their name and the area/department they work in. This ensures that access control is maintained as well as specific protocols for areas that are at a higher risk (cash vaults, administrative areas, staff only restrooms etc.).

Parking Lot Safety

If possible, travel to and from work and parking areas with other people. Park in areas that are patrolled and well lighted after dark. Use security escorts during off-hours when others are not around.

Also keep in mind:

Lighting: Always choose well-lighted parking areas. Be aware of your surroundings!

Don't Sit: Don't loiter in the parking lot. Take care of phone calls and other matters inside the location you are going to. Always turn off the ignition, remove the key, and lock your car doors, no matter how soon you plan on returning.

Valuables: Keep valuables and packages locked in the trunk. If you are carrying packages, try to keep one hand free, even if it means making an extra trip.

Approaching: Be alert as you approach your car in the parking area. Pay attention to nearby vehicles, individuals and hiding areas that criminals might use, such as under the car or in the back seat. Your keys and cell phone should be in hand or at reach. Always look around before you get in or out of your car.

Buddy System: Always walk in groups when possible. Safety in numbers!

Security Escort: Get a security escort if available.

Who's next to you? Assess who you are next to when parking your car, and when coming back to your vehicle. If possible, do not park next to vans, trucks with campers or other vehicles whose size and structure can provide concealment for a potential assailant.

Parking Garages: Exercise caution and be extra alert when using underground or enclosed parking garages. Walk in the center aisle, rather than close to parked cars. If you have a choice, park in areas that have an attendant, or in locations that have heavy pedestrian traffic. Have your key in hand before you get to your car and be aware of occupied cars around you.

Disabled Car: Criminals have been known to disable a car by flattening a tire to strand their victim. The victim is then approached, offered assistance, and attacked. If your car is disabled in suspicious circumstances and a stranger offers to help you, escape the area and scream loud and long. Report to security or police immediately.

Telephone Safety

Cell Phones: Cell phones are a great tool for alerting others in almost every environment. Program numbers into your cell phone so that they are easily found and used. Some agencies use mass alert text messaging.

Threatening Calls: If you receive a threatening, harassing or obscene telephone call, notify security or police, your supervisor, and the telephone company.

Keep Records: Keep a record of the date, time and the content of each threatening, harassing or obscene telephone call for security or police and the telephone company. In some cases, cell phone companies can block callers who are threatening and harassing.

Emergency Numbers: What are yours? Memorize numbers for emergency codes, police, security, fire, etc. Post the numbers near every telephone or on your person.

Follow "Emergency Codes" response protocols:
(See Chapter 13)

Practice Emergency Numbers: Rehearse mentally and physically (turn phone off when practicing) calls you would make to police, fire, emergency personnel or anyone who would respond to your situation. Considering your stress level response, this skill could save your life.

ICE = In Case of Emergency: Program your cell phone with ICE numbers should you be unable to make a call yourself. Multiple ICE numbers can be added to your cell phone address book. Label them as ICE-1, ICE-2 etc.

Emergency Phones: Emergency phones can alert security personnel to your situation. Blue emergency phones are commonly found in parking structures and lots.

Consider all these factors when thinking about how your work environment will contribute to your safety, or make you unsafe. Also, consider some of the simplest things: your workplace is filled with numerous obstacles that can inhibit your ability to escape a situation. Some common obstacles that can be trip hazards are chairs, people, walls, tables, cars, curbs, trees, inclement weather, machines, desks, spills on the floor, etc. Be aware of changes in your environment that might inhibit your ability to escape a potentially violent incident.

Chapter 13

Emergency Codes & Procedures

"Be Prepared... the meaning of the motto is that a scout must prepare himself by previous thinking out and practicing how to act on any accident or emergency so that he is never taken by surprise."

- Sir Robert Baden-Powell, British Army Officer, founder of the Boy Scouts (1857-1941)

The use of codes is intended to convey essential information quickly and with a minimum of misunderstanding to staff, while preventing stress or panic among guests and visitors to the workplace. Emergency codes are frequently coded by color, and the color codes denote different events at different corporations and are not always universal.

Fire Code provides an appropriate response in the event of an actual or suspected fire in order to protect life, property and vital services.

Medical Code provides an appropriate response to a suspected or imminent medical emergency for a guest or staff person.

Lost Person Code provides an appropriate response in the event a lost person or possible child abduction from the facility.

The following is particular to health care facilities facing infant abductions:

Listed below are characteristics of a typical abductor as identified by the National Center for Missing and Exploited Children (NCMEC). However, there is no guarantee an infant abductor will fit this description, and anyone acting suspicious in areas of risk for abductions should be reported immediately.

- Female of "childbearing" age (range from 12-50), often overweight.
- Most likely compulsive; most often relies on manipulation, lying, and deception.
- Frequently indicates that she has lost a baby or is incapable of having one.
- Often married or cohabitating; companion's desire for a child or the abductor's desire to provide her companion with "his" child may be the motivation for the abduction.
- Usually lives in the community where the abduction takes place.
- Frequently initially visits the nursery and maternity units at more than one healthcare facility prior to the abduction; asks detailed questions about procedures and the maternity floor layout; frequently uses a fire exit stairwell for escape; and may also try to abduct from the home setting.
- Usually plans the abduction, but does not necessarily target a specific infant; frequently seizes on any opportunity present.
- Frequently impersonates a nurse or other allied childcare personnel.

- Often becomes familiar with staff, staff work routines, and the victim's parents.
- Demonstrates a capability to provide "good" care to the baby once the abduction occurs.
- May remove the newborn as follows: carrying the infant, carrying a bag large enough to hold an infant, covering the infant with coat/baby blanket, or may be in healthcare/ childcare uniform/scrubs carrying the infant.

Robbery Code provides an appropriate response in the event of an armed or unarmed robbery. Businesses that handle money, deal with prescription pharmaceuticals or sell high-end items are at risk of a robbery.

AVADE® Robbery Prevention & Response Guidelines

Robbery is the crime of seizing property through violence or intimidation. A perpetrator of a robbery is a robber. Because violence is an ingredient of most robberies, they may result in the harm or murder of their victims.

Robbers want your money or property, and they want it quickly. Robbery is a risky business and robbers are usually nervous. You do not want to delay a robbery in any way—it increases the potential for violence. Give the robber what he or she wants and do it quickly. Do not risk your life, or another person's life for property.

Robberies occur at predictable times. Opening and closing periods are particularly vulnerable times due to low staffing and large amounts of cash on hand. Robberies increase during the holiday season due to the increased cash volume and the presence of large crowds that distract and preoccupy store and company personnel.

Report suspicious activity. If you observe an individual(s) or occupied vehicle lingering around your business for a time, or in a manner that makes you suspicious or uncomfortable, write down the license number, color and make of the car, description of the individual(s) and call police or security. Many robbers like to watch and wait for the right opportunity.

PREVENTION - Security Devices

(see Chapter 12: Environmental Factors)

- Control access to areas where cash or other valuable items are stored.
- CCTV is a great deterrent against criminals.
- Signage inside and outside will emphasize your security policy on limited cash on hand and/or employee inaccessibility to the safe.
- Silent "hold-up" or "panic" alarms should be considered.

PREVENTION - Identification

Greet each customer. Establish eye contact and remember their general appearance. Good customer service discourages hesitant robbers as well as other thieves. This attention to detail conveys control and puts people on notice they have been observed and can be identified later.

Place height markings along the vertical frame at the entrance. This gives employees the ability to tell how tall the robber is at a glance, so they can tell the authorities.

PREVENTION - Policy Considerations

Recognize your potential for being held up. Work with local police and crime prevention specialists. Preventive strategies are as much their concern and responsibility as apprehension of criminals.

- Check references of prospective employees. Do a background check of their previous employers.
- Keep a file on all employees, including their pictures. Past employees know store procedure and where money is kept.
- Re-key locks, and reset codes and combinations when affected employees are dismissed for cause.
- Establish clear and consistent policies regarding money in the till. Establish how much money will be kept in the till, what bill denominations employees will accept, how to respond to "suspicious" inquires, and how to handle loiterers. All employees should be trained and given a written description of store policy.
- Maintain adequate staff levels. Be especially careful during opening and closing periods, lunch hours, and holiday seasons when there is more money on-site and more distractions.
- As an employee, your commitment to security procedures will reduce the risk of criminal confrontation and physical harm.

Robbery Prevention

When to Call Emergency Numbers

- A crime is in progress
- A situation is about to escalate into an emergency (endangering life or major property)
- A crime has just occurred (remember description of suspect and direction in which he or she fled)

Be Alert

- Pay attention to who is in your work area, and know who belongs in your work area. Become familiar with the faces of people who belong in your building. Pay attention to people who behave suspiciously, i.e. someone who loiters in the area with no apparent purpose. Be particularly aware of a person you have seen loitering more than once.

PREVENTION - Design Considerations

- Use gates and counters to separate clients from employees when appropriate.
- Post signs to designate restricted areas: "Private" or "Employees Only."
- Install an information desk and staff it during business hours. It will provide some surveillance of the main entrance of the building.
- Create transition zones. These can be steps up or down, screened or partitioned off areas, different levels of lighting or carpeting in a given space. These methods subtly indicate a change in usage from public to private.
- Report any broken lights, flickering lights, broken locks or doors, dimly lit corridors, doors that don't lock properly, broken windows, or lock devices to management or security immediately. Not attending to these items can create an environment conducive to crime. The faster they are repaired the safer the environment will be.

PREVENTION - Business Security Procedures

Develop company security procedures. The procedures should state the company's policy and dedication to a crime-and-violence-free workplace. Including procedures for the following will help empower employees to make their workplace safe and crime-free.

- Dealing with trespassers and/or difficult people
- Opening and closing the office
- Using the office during off hours
- Recommendations for personal property security
- Who to report crimes and suspicious activities to
- Emergency exit plan

Response During the Robbery

- Remain calm. Most robbers do not wish to harm their victims. They are only interested in getting money or property. The calmer you are, the less chance that the robber becomes agitated or dangerous. This also increases your chances of getting a more accurate description of the robber, which may aid in the robber's apprehension.
- Do not argue, fight, surprise or attempt to use weapons against a robber. He has already taken a major risk by entering your business and is usually as frightened as you are. Because of this, additional provocation on your part could make the situation worse. Therefore, give the robber exactly what he or she wants and do it quickly. Don't take unnecessary chances with your life!
- While you should cooperate with robbers, don't volunteer any assistance. Don't give all the money if the robber only asks for twenty-dollar bills.
- Activate silent alarms/security devices if you can do this without detection.

- Watch the robber's hands. If the robber is not wearing any gloves, anything he touches might leave good fingerprints.
- Give the robber your "bait" money. Be sure to inform the investigating officer that you did so.
- Be systematic in your observations. Look the robber over carefully. Mentally note as many details as possible until you can write them down. Compare the robber with yourself. Is he taller, heavier, older, etc.?
- Notice the type and description of any weapons used. Glance at the weapon only long enough to identify it. Look at the robber from then on. Make no sudden moves and don't be heroic!
- Observe the direction the robber takes in leaving the scene. If a vehicle is involved, make note of the make, model, year, color, license plate number and issuing state.

Response After the Robbery

Telephone police immediately. If you act quickly, police might be able to catch the suspect and recover your money. When you dial 9-1-1, the procedure is always the same. You will be asked if your emergency involves police, fire or medical. Request police. Lock all doors and allow no one in. Ask witnesses to remain on the premises until police arrive. Do not touch anything the robber may have touched. Do not discuss what happened with any other witnesses. Your own impressions should be kept untainted until you have talked with authorities.

Complete your post-incident documentation. Be as complete as possible. Police may want a copy of your report. (See Chapter 7 for post incident documentation procedures.)

Provide incident debriefing. (See Chapter 8 for critical incident stress debriefing.)

Robbery response strategies require planning and coordination between employees and management. Give some thought to how you might react in a robbery situation and discuss your concerns with co-workers and employers. Common sense, caution and adherence to established policies and procedures can reduce the amount of money stolen and minimize the chance for injury and loss of life.

Bomb Threat Code provides an appropriate response in the event of a bomb threat or the discovery of a suspicious device/package.

Combative Person Code provides an appropriate response to situations involving an aggressive/hostile/combative or potentially combative person.

Recognizing Early Warning Signs. Combative Person or Potentially Combative Person Symptoms include:

No single sign alone should cause concern, but a combination of any of the following signs should be cause for concern and action:

- Direct or verbal threats of harm.
- Intimidation of others by words and or actions.
- Refusing to follow policies.
- Hypersensitivity or extreme suspiciousness.
- Extreme moral righteousness.
- Inability to take criticism regarding job performance.
- Holding a grudge, especially against a supervisor.

- Repeatedly verbalizing that something will happen to the other person against whom the individual has the grudge. Expression of extreme desperation over recent problems.
- Intentional disregard for the safety of others.
- Destruction of property.

For more Combative/Assaultive Behaviors see Chapter 6.

To avoid a threatening or escalated response by the aggressive individual proper positioning of the team is crucial. Team cornering of an aggressive individual may escalate the situation.

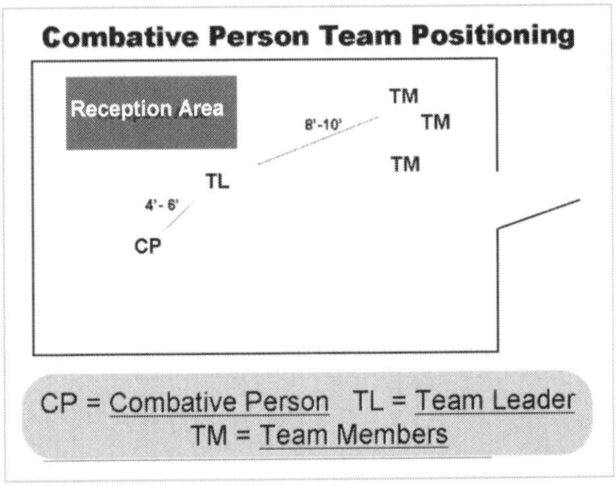

Active Shooter Code provides an appropriate response in the event of an incident involving a person with a weapon or who has taken hostages within the facility.

This is the most extreme incidence of violence in today's society—the active shooter who enters one's home, work, school, place of worship or public place and opens fire on innocent people, causing death and serious bodily injury.

What we know about active shooters:

- The active shooter is acting alone 98% of the time.
- He is suicidal 90% of the time, usually commits suicide on-site.
- He almost never takes hostages, nor has any interest in negotiating. Is preoccupied with a high body count, which is almost always his one and only goal.
- Active-shooters race to murder everybody they reach in an effort to avoid contact with police.
- Most incidents are over within four minutes or less!
- Shooter usually has multiple weapons and an ability to reload his weapons several times.
- Long arms (rifles/shotguns) are involved 80% of the time.
- High prediction of serious injury to the innocent and unarmed.
- At least 50% of the time, the person stopping the incident is non-police.

Surviving and Active Shooter

- Escape if safe to do so!
- Hide and cover in place if you cannot escape.
- Alert authorities—police, security.
- Locks doors in your immediate area.
- Place barriers and remain absolutely quiet.
- If escape is not possible and danger is imminent, attack the attacker.
- When law enforcement arrives, go face down on ground with palms up.

Awareness and vigilance play the most important role in overall prevention and intervention of violence. When faced with imminent danger, one must realize that mental strength will be absolutely necessary to stay alive and survive.

Hazmat Code provides an appropriate response to an actual or suspected hazardous material spill or release in a manner that is safe for staff, guests and visitors.

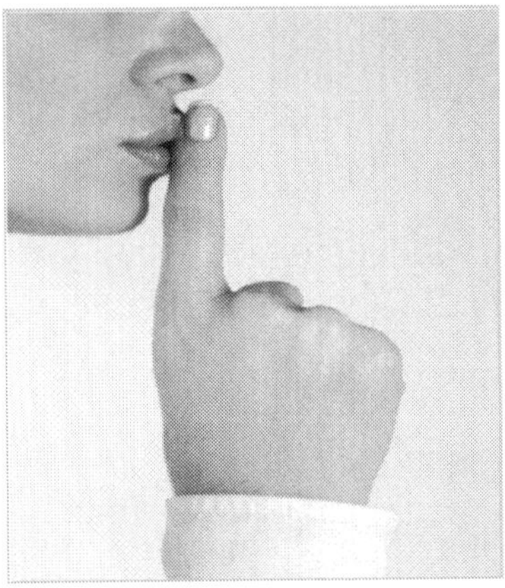

Personal Codes for Alerting Others provide a quick, non-attention-getting communication to security or other responders of a possible threatening, emergent or imminent situation. Using personal codes between team members can alert help without alerting the assailant that you are requesting assistance/help.

Conclusion

Workplace violence is, unfortunately, on the rise. But by studying the AVADE® strategies, learning them, integrating them and teaching them to your co-workers, you can lessen your chances of being a victim of workplace violence.

Learn the AVADE® principles for defusing tense situations. Learn to identify the signs and symptoms of potential violence. Above all, learn to trust your instincts, and listen to your intuition. Remember, your best tool for keeping yourself safe is your own mind.

Bibliography and Reference Guide

Books, CD's, DVD's and Websites

Adams, Terry and Rob. *Seminar Production Business: Your Step by Step Guide to Success*. Entrepreneur Press, Canada 2003.

Amdur, Ellis. *Dueling with O-sensei: Grappling with the Myth of the Warrior Sage.* Edgework, Seattle, WA 2000.

Andersen, Peter A. *The Complete Idiot's Guide to Body Language.* Alpha Books, Indianapolis, IN 2004.

Andrews, Andy. *The Travelers Gift: Seven Decisions that Determine Personal Success.* Nelsen Books, Nashville, Tennessee, 2002.

Arapakis, Maria. *Soft Power: How to Speak Up, Set Limits, and Say No Without Losing Your Lover, Your Job, or Your Friends*. Warner Books, Inc., NY, NY 1990.

Artwhohl, Alexis & Christensen, Loren. *Deadly Force Encounters: What Cops need to know to mentally and physically prepare for and survive a gunfight*. Paladin Press, Boulder, CO 1997.

ASIS International. *Security Management Magazine.* www.securitymanagment.com 2006-2009.

Bloodworth, Venice. *Key to Yourself: Opening the Door to a Joyful Life from Within.* DeVorrs Publication, Marina Del Ray, CA 1953.

Brown, Tom. *Survival Guides: Americas Bestselling Wilderness Series.* Berkley Books, New York, 1984.

Byrnes, John D. *Before Conflict: Preventing Aggressive Behavior*. Scarecrow Press, Lanham, Maryland and Oxford 2002.

Canfield, Jack and Switzer, Janet. *The Success Principles: How to Get from Where You Are to Where You Want to Be*. Harper Collins Publishers, NY, NY 2005.

Canfield, Jack and Bunch, Jim. *The Ultimate Life Workshop: 7 Strategies for Creating the Ultimate Life*. Live Workshop, February 2008.

Carnegie, Dale. *Golden Book*. www.dalecarnegie.com.
Carnegie, Dale. *How to Win Friends & Influence People*. Pocket Books, NY, NY 1936.

Chodron, Thubten. *Working With Anger*. Snow Lion Publication, Ithaca, NY 2001.

Christensen, Loren. *The Way Alone: Your Path to Excellence in the Martial Arts*. Paladin Press, Boulder, CO 1987.

Christensen, Loren. *Warriors: On Living with Courage, Discipline and Honor*. Paladin Press, Boulder, CO 2004.

Covey, Stephen R. *The 7 Habits of Highly Effective People: Powerful Lessons in Personal Change*. Fireside, NY, NY 1989.

Covey, Stephen R. *The 8th Habit: From Effectiveness to Greatness*. Better Life Media, DVD and CD, 2004.

Day Laura, *Practical Intuition*. Villard Books, NY, NY 1996.

DeBecker, Gavin. *The Gift of Fear*. Dell Publishing, NY, NY 1997.

DeBecker, Gavin. *Fear Less: Real Truth about Risk, Safety, and Security in a Time of Terrorism.* Little Brown and Company, Boston, NY, London 2002.

DeBecker, Gavin & Taylor, Tom & Marquart, Jeff. *Just 2 Seconds: Using Time and Space to Defeat Assassins.* The Gavin DeBecker Center for the Study and Reduction of Violence a not-for-profit foundation, Studio City, CA 2008.

DeBecker, Gavin. *Protecting the Gift: Keeping Children and Teenagers Safe (and Parents Sane).* A Dell Trade Paperback, NY, NY 1999.

Deshimaru, Taisen. *The Zen Way to the Martial Arts: A Japanese Master Reveals the Secrets of the Samurai.* Penguin Compass. NY, NY 1982.

DeMasco, Steve. *The Shaolin Way: 10 Modern Secrets of Survival from a Shaolin Kung Fu Grandmaster.* Harper, NY, NY 2006.

Dreher, Diane. *The Tao if Inner Peace.* Harper Perennial, NY, NY 1990.

Dyer, Wayne. *The Power of Intention; Learning to Co-Create your world your way.* Hay House, CA 2004.

Eckman, Paul. *Emotions Revealed: Recognizing Faces and Feelings to Improve Communication and Emotional Life.* Henry Holt & Company, NY, NY 2007.

Eckman, Paul. *Telling Lies.* WW. Norton Company, NY and London 1991.

Fowler, David. *Be Safe Not Sorry, the Art and Science of keeping YOU and your family Safe from Crime and Violence.* Personal Safety Training Inc., Coeur d Alene, ID 2011.

Funakoshi, Gichen. *Karate-Do My Way of Life.* Kodansha International, Tokyo, NY. London, 1975.

Gallo, Carmine. *Inspire Your Audience: 7 Keys to Influential Presentations.* Paper. Communication Skills Coach, Author of *Fire Them Up!*

Garner, Bryan. *Black's Law Dictionary: Seventh Edition.* West Group, St. Paul, MI, 1999.

Gawain, Shakti. *Creative Visualization.* New World Library, Novato, CA 2002.

Gawain, Shakti. *Developing Intuition: Practical Guide for Daily Life.* New World Library, Novato, CA 2000.

Gladwell, Malcolm. *Blink.* Little, Brown & Company, NY 2005.

Goleman, Daniel. *Emotional Intelligence.* Bantam Books, NY, NY 2005.

Gray, John. *Beyond Mars and Venus.* Better Life Media, DVD and CD, 2004.

Gregory, Hamilton. *Public Speaking for College and Career: Fifth Edition.* McGraw-Hill, Boston 1999.

Gross, Linden. *Surviving A Stalker: Everything you need to know to keep yourself safe. Marlowe and Company,* NY, NY 2000.

Grossman, Dave & Christensen, Loren. *On Combat: The Psychology of Deadly Conflict in War and Peace.* PPCT Research, IL 2004.

Grossman, Dave & DeGaetano, Gloria. *Stop Teaching our Kids to*

Kill: A call to action against TV, Movie & Video Game Violence. Crown Publishers, NY, NY 1999.

Harrell, Keith. *Attitude is Everything: 10 Life Changing Steps to Turning Attitude Into Action.* Harper Collins Publishing, NY, NY 1999.

Hawkins, David R, MD. *Power vs. Force: The Hidden Determinants of Human Behavior.* Veritas, Sedona, AZ 2004.

Headley, Steve. *Assault Prevention Workshop.* Assault Prevention Workshops, LLC 2009.

Hyams, Joe. *Zen in the Martial Arts.* Bantam Books, Toronto, NY, London, Sydney, Auckland, 1982.

IAHSS. *Basic Training Manual and Study Guide for Healthcare Security Officers.* Lombard, IL 1995.

IAHSS. *Journal of Healthcare Protection Management.* Bayside, NY 2008.

Jo-Ellan Dimitrius, Ph.D., and Mark Mazzarella. *Reading People: How to Understand people and Predict their Behavior-Anytime, Anyplace.* Ballantine Books, NY, NY 1999.

Kane, Lawrence A. *Surviving Armed Assaults.* YMAA Publication Center, Boston MA 2006.

Kim, Daeshik and Leland, Tom. *Exploring Sport Karate.* Wm. C Brown Company Publishers, Dubuque, IA 1971.

Krebs & Henry & Gabriele. *When Violence Erupts: A Survival Guide for Emergency Responders.* The C.V. Mosby Company, St.

Louis, Baltimore, Philadelphia, Toronto, 1990.

Lawler, Jennifer. *Dojo Wisdom: 100 Simple Ways to Become a Stronger, Calmer, more Courageous Person.* Penguin Compass, NY, NY 2003.

Lee, Bruce. *Tao of Jeet Kune Do.* Ohara Publications, Santa Clarita, CA 1975.

Lee, Linda. *The Bruce Lee Story.* Ohara Publications, Santa Clarita, CA 1989.

Lion, John, MD. *Evaluation and Management of the Violent Patient: Guidelines in the Hospital and Institution.* Charles C. Thomas Publisher, Springfield, IL 1972.

Little, John. *The Warrior Within: The philosophies of Bruce Lee to better understand the world around you and achieve a rewarding life.* Contemporary Books, Chicago, IL 1996.

Machowicz, Richard J. *Unleash The Warrior Within: Develop the Focus, Discipline, Confidence and Courage You Need to Achieve Unlimited Goals.* Marlowe & Company, NY 2002.

Mackay, Harvey. *Harvey Mackay's Column This Week.* Weekly e-mail publication, www.harveymackay.com.

MacYoung, Marc "Animal." *Ending Violence Quickly: How Bouncers, Bodyguards and Other Security Professionals Handle Ugly Situations.* Paladin Press, Boulder, CO 1993.

Maggio, Rosalie. *How to Say It: Choice Words, Phrases, Sentences, and Paragraphs for Every Situation.* Prentice Hall Press, NY, NY 2001.

Maltz, Maxwell MD. *Psycho-Cybernetics: A New Way to Get More Living Out Of Life.* Essandress, NY, NY 1960.

Marcinko, Richard. *The Rogue Warriors Strategy For Success.* Pocket Books, NY, NY 1997.

Mason, Tom & Chandley Mark. *Managing Violence and Aggression: A Manual for Nurses and Health Care Workers.* Churchill Livingstone, Edinburgh, 1999.

McGrew, James. *Think Safe: Practical Measures to Increase Security at Home, at Work, and Throughout Life.* Cameo Publications, Hilton Head Island, SC 2004.

McTaggart, Lynne. *The Intention Experiment: Using Your thoughts to Change Your Life and the World.* Free Press, NY, NY 2007.

Medina, John. *Brain Rules: 12 Principles for Surviving and Thriving at Work, Home, and School.* Pear Press, Seattle, WA 2008.

Morgenstern, Julie. *Never Check E-Mail in the Morning.* Simon & Schuster, NY, London, Toronto, Sydney 2005.

Murphy, Joseph, Dr. *The Power of Your Subconscious Mind.* Bantam Books, NY, Toronto, London, Sidney, Auckland 2000.

Musashi, Miyamoto. Translated by Thomas Cleary. *The Book of Five Rings.* Shambala, Boston and London 2003.

Norris, Chuck. *The Secret Power Within: Zen Solutions to Real Problems.* Broadway Books, NY 1996.

Norris, Chuck. *Winning Tournament Karate.* Ohara Publications, Burbank, CA 1975.

Nowicki, Ed. *Total Survival.* Performance Dimensions, Powers Lake, MI 1993.

Ouellette, Roland W. *Management of Aggressive Behavior.* Performance Dimension Publishing, Powers Lake, WI 1993.

Palumbo, Dennis. *The Secrets of Hakkoryu Jujutsu: Shodan Tactics.* Paladin Press Boulder, CO 1987.

Parker, S.L. *212 the extra degree.* The Walk the Talk Co. 2005 www.walkthetalk.com.

Patire, Tom. *Tom Patire's Personal Protection Handbook.* Three Rivers Press, NY 2003.

Peale, Norman Vincent. *Six Attitudes for Winners.* Tyndale House Publishers, Inc. Wheaton, Il 1989.

Peale, Norman Vincent. *The Power of Positive Thinking.* Ballantine Books, NY, NY 1956.

Pease, Allan and Barbara. *The Definitive Book of Body Language.* Bantam Dell. NY, NY 2004.

Perkins, John & Ridenhour, Al and Kovsky Matt. *Attack Proof: The Ultimate Guide to Personal Protection.* Human Kinetics, Champaign, IL 2000.

PPCT Management Systems, Inc. *Defensive Tactics Instructor Manual.* PPCT 2005.

Purpura, Philip. *The Security Handbook: Second Edition.* Butterworth Heinemann, Boston, 2003.

Rail, Robert R. *The Unspoken Dialogue: Understanding Body Language and Controlling Interviews and Negotiations*. Varro Press, Kansas City 2001

Ralston, Peter. *Cheng Hsin: The Principles of Effortless Power.* North Atlantic Books, Berkeley, CA 1989.

Ratey, John J. *Spark: The Revolutionary New Science of Exercise and the Brain.* Little, Brown and Co., NY, NY 2008.

Rodale Inc. *Men's Health Today 2007*. Rodale Inc. US 2007.

Strong, Sanford. *Strong on Defense: Survival Rules to Protect You and Your Family from Crime.* Pocket Books, NY, NY 1996.

Sjodin, Terri. *New Sales Speak: The 9 Biggest Sales Presentation Mistakes and How to Avoid Them*. Better Life Media. DVD and CD 2004.

Soo, Chee, *The Chinese Art of T'ai Chi Ch'uan: The Taoist way to mental and physical health.* The Aquarian Press, Wellingborough, Northamptonshire 1984.

Staley, Charles. *The Science of Martial Arts Training.* Multi Media Books, Burbank, CA 1999.

The Results Driven Manager. *Dealing with Difficult People*. Harvard Business School Publishing Corp, Boston MA 2005.

Theriault, Jean Yves. *Full Contact Karate.* Contemporary Books Inc. Chicago, 1983.

The World's Greatest Treasury of Health Secrets. Bottom Line Publications, Stamford, CT 2006.

Thompson, George. *Verbal Judo.* Quill William Morrow, NY 1993.

Tolle, Eckhart. *Practicing The Power of Now: Essential Teachings, Meditations, and Exercises from the Power of Now.* New World Library, Novato, CA 1999.

Tolle, Eckhart. *The Power of Now.* New World Library, Novato, CA 2004.

Tsunetomo, Yamamoto. *Hagakure: The Book of the Samurai.* Kodansha International, Tokyo, NY, London 1979.

Turner, James T. *Violence in the Medical Care Setting.* Aspen Systems Corporation, Rockville, MD 1984.

Tzu, Sun. *The Art of War.* Samuel Griffith Interpretation, Oxford University Press, 1993.

Uchiyama, Kosho. *Opening the Hand of Thought: Foundations of Zen Buddhist Practice.* Wisdom Publications, Boston 2004.

Ueshiba, Kisshomaru. *The Spirit of Aikido.* Kodansha International, Tokyo, NY, London, 1987.

US Dept. of Justice. *Workplace Violence: Issues in Response.* Critical Incident Response Group, National Center for the Analysis of Violent Crime, FBI Academy, Quantico, Virginia 2001.

Wallace, Bill. *The Ultimate Kick: The Wallace Method to Winning Karate.* Unique Publications, Burbank, CA 1987.

Webster, Noah. *Webster's Dictionary.* Modern Promotions Publishers, NY, NY 1984.

Websites

http://www.AVADEtraining.com

http://www.personalsafetytraining.com

http://www.socstraining.com

http://www.aaets.org/article54.htm

http://en.wikipedia.org/wiki/Excited_delirium

http://en.wikipedia.org/wiki/Chemical_restraint

http://www.aele.org/law/2008ALL12/chicago.pdf

http://www.hospitalmedicine.org/AM/Template.cfm?Section=Reference_Material&Template=/CM/ContentDisplay.cfm&ContentID=17070

Workplace Violence:
http://cms.nursingworld.org/workplaceviolence

http://helpguide.org/mental/eq4_emotion_communicates.htm

http://hawaii.gov/ag/cpja/quicklinks/workplace_violence/WVfull.pdf

http://www.ena.org/media/PressReleases/Pages/WorkPlaceViolence.aspx

http://www.jointcommission.org/SentinelEvents/SentinelEventAlert/sea_40.htm

http://www.dli.mn.gov/Wsc/PDF/WorkplaceViolencePreventionGuide.pdf

http://www.cbs.state.or.us/external/osha/pdf/workshops/702w.pdf

http://blog.awareity.com/2010/03/04/identifying-red-flags-warning-signs-and-indicators/

http://www.co.midland.tx.us/edp/pdf_files/Misc/Workplace%20-%20Violence.pdf

A Circle of Distortion: The Social Construction of Mass Murder in the United States by Grant Duwe
http://wcr.sonoma.edu/v6n1/manuscripts/duwe.pdf

Active Shooter: How To Respond
http://www.alerts.si.edu/docs/DHS_ActiveShooterBook.pdf

Active Shooter: Recommendations and Analysis for Risk Mitigation
http://www.nypdshield.org/public/SiteFiles/documents/ActiveShooter.pdf

ASIS International Active Shooter resource page
http://www.asisonline.org/education/activeShooter.xml

ASIS/SHRM Workplace Violence Prevention and Intervention Standard
http://www.abdi-secure-ecommerce.com/asis/ps-1092-30-1967.aspx

Current Intelligence Bulletin #57: Violence in the Workplace: Risk Factors and Prevention Strategies
http://www.cdc.gov/niosh/docs/96-100/

Effectiveness of Crime Prevention Through Environmental Design (CPTED) in Reducing Robberies, by Carri Casteel, MPH, Corinne Peek-Asa, PhD
http://www.usak.org.tr/istanbul/files/cr.pr.environmental.design.pdf

Effectiveness of Safety Measures Recommended for Prevention of Workplace Homicide, by Dana Loomis, PhD; Stephen W. Marshall, PhD; Susanne H. Wolf, RN, MPH; Carol W. Runyan, PhD; John D. Butts, MD

http://jama.jamanetwork.com/article.aspx?articleid=194680

Enforcement Procedures for Investigating or Inspecting Workplace Violence Incidents CPL 02-01-052
http://www.osha.gov/OshDoc/Directive_pdf/CPL_02-01-052.pdf

Fatal occupational injuries by industry and event or exposure, All United States, 2009
http://www.bls.gov/iif/oshwc/cfoi/cftb0241.pdf

FEMA EMI IS-907 - Active Shooter: What You Can Do
http://training.fema.gov/EMIWeb/IS/is907.asp
Guidelines for Preventing Workplace Violence for Health Care & Social Service Workers
http://www.osha.gov/Publications/osha3148.pdf

Number and percent distribution of nonfatal occupational injuries and illnesses involving days away from work by event or exposure leading to injury or illness and number of days away from work, private industry, 2009
http://www.bls.gov/iif/oshwc/osh/case/ostb2516.pdfhttp://www.bls.gov/iif/oshwc/osh/case/ostb2516.pdf

Occupational homicides by selected characteristics, 1997-2010
http://www.bls.gov/iif/oshwc/cfoi/work_hom.pdf

Occupational Suicides: Census of Fatal Occupational Injuries Fact Sheet, August 2009 http://bls.gov/iif/oshwc/cfoi/osar0010.pdf

OSHA Workplace Violence
http://www.osha.gov/SLTC/workplaceviolence/

Recommendations for Workplace Violence Prevention Programs in Late-Night Retail Establishments - OSHA Publication 3153
http://www.osha.gov/Publications/osha3153.pdf

Revisions to the 2009 Census of Fatal Occupational Injuries (CFOI) counts http://www.bls.gov/iif/oshwc/cfoi/cfoi_revised09.pdf

Summary of Research on Mass Murder by John Klofas http://www.rit.edu/cla/cpsi/WorkingPapers/2009/2009-11.pdf

Ten Tips to Mitigate Workplace Violence and Threats, by Felix P. Nater http://www.securitymagazine.com/articles/83329-10-tips-to-mitigate-workplace-violence-and-threats

The Psychology of Security, by Bruce Schneier http://www.schneier.com/essay-155.html

The Workplace Violence Prevention eReport http://www.workplaceviolence911.com/preventionreport

U.S. BLS Census of Fatal Occupational Injuries (CFOI) 2009 Chart Pack http://www.bls.gov/iif/oshwc/cfoi/cfch0008.pdf

U.S. BLS Census of Fatal Occupational Injuries (CFOI) 2010 Chart Pack http://www.bls.gov/iif/oshwc/cfoi/cfch0009.pdf

U.S. BLS Fatal occupational injuries by selected characteristics: State of incident, employee status, sex, age, race, event or exposure, source, secondary source, nature, part of body, worker activity, location, occupation, and industry, 1992-2002 (revised final counts) http://www.bls.gov/iif/oshwc/cfoi/cftb0186.pdf

U.S. BLS Table 4, Number, incidence rate, and median days away from work for nonfatal occupational injuries and illnesses involving days away from work by selected detailed occupation and private industry, state government, and local government, 2010 http://www.bls.gov/news.release/osh2.t04.htm

Violence in the Workplace by Tanya Restrepo and Harry Shuford https://www.ncci.com/documents/Workplace_Research.pdf

When Prevention Fails: Minimizing the Post-Incident Impact of Workplace Violence http://www.businessinsurance.com/section/NEWS050106

Workplace violence intervention effectiveness: A systematic literature review, by James T. Wassell
http://www.sciencedirect.com/science/article/pii/S092575350800218X

Workplace Violence Prevention: Readiness and Response, by Stephen J. Romano, Micòl E. Levi-Minzi, Eugene A. Rugala and Vincent B. Van Hasselt http://www.fbi.gov/stats-services/ publications/law-enforcementbulletin/january2011/ workplace_violence_prevention

Workplace Violence, 1993-2009 National Crime Victimization Survey and the Census of Fatal Occupational Injuries
http://bjs.ojp.usdoj.gov/content/pub/pdf/wv09.pdf

Workplace Violence: Issues in Response, Edited by Eugene A. Rugala and Arnold R. Isaacs
http://www.fbi.gov/stats-services/publications/workplace-violence

Work-related Homicides: The Facts by Eric Sygnatur and Guy Toscano http://www.bls.gov/opub/cwc/archive/spring2000art1.pdf

Work-related multiple-fatality incidents, by Dino Drudi and Mark Zak http://www.bls.gov/mlr/2004/10/art2full.pdf

About the Author

David Fowler is the founder and president of (PSTI) Personal Safety Training Incorporated and AVADE Training LLC located in Coeur d' Alene, ID. He is responsible for the overall management and operations of PSTI and AVADE, which offers seminars, training, consulting, and protective details. Since 1990, David has been involved security operations, training, and protective details.

He is the author of the SOCS® (Security Oriented Customer Service) program and training manual as well as the AVADE® (Personal Safety Training and Workplace Violence Prevention) programs and training manuals. He is also the author of *Be Safe Not Sorry: the art and science of keeping YOU and your family safe from crime and violence*. David has worked with thousands of individuals and hundreds of agencies and corporations throughout the United States and Canada. His presentations have included international, national and local seminars. David's thorough understanding of safety and security, and martial science add an exciting and interesting approach to his style of presentation.

David is a certified master instructor in several nationally recognized training programs such as Workplace Violence Prevention (AVADE®), OC Pepper Aerosol Training, Tactical Handcuffing, Security Oriented Customer Service (SOCS®), Defensive Tactics

(DTS™), Defense Baton™, Security Incident Reporting System (SIRS™), Code Gray Training™ and AVADE® Personal Safety Training. David has certified and trained thousands of individuals in these programs and others throughout the United States and abroad.

He is a Graduate of (ESI) Executive Security International's advanced Executive Protection Program and the Protective Intelligence and Investigations program. A member of ASIS (American Society for Industrial Security), The International Law Enforcement Educators & Trainers Association (ILEETA) and the International Association of Healthcare Safety & Security (IAHSS).

David brings insight, experience, and a passion for empowering people and organizations, utilizing the training programs and protective services that he offers here in the United States and in other countries. He is considered by many to be the most dynamic and motivational speaker and trainer in the security and personal safety industry.

David is happily married to the love of his life, Genelle Fowler. They live in Coeur d' Alene, ID and have five children and one grandchild. David and Genelle have committed their lives to serving others through the mission of safety. Both David and Genelle travel extensively providing training and consulting to corporations throughout North America.

Training Courses For YOU And Your Agency

The only way to deal with conflict and avoid violence of any type is through awareness, knowledge, defensive training and escape planning.

David Fowler, President of PSTI (Personal Safety Training Incorporated) specializes in nationally recognized training programs which empower individuals, increase confidence and promote pro-active preventative solutions.

OSHA, Labor & Industries, Joint Commission, State WPV Laws, and the Deptment of Health all recognize that programs like PSTI's are excellent preventive measures to reduce crime, violence and aggression in the workplace.

PSTI Offers

- On-Site Training
- Instructor Seminars
- Train-the-Trainer
- Combo Classes
- Scenario Training
- Books and CD's
- Videos and DVD's

On-Site Training (we will come to you!) No need to send staff away for training. PSTI will come to your place of business and train your staff.

AVADE® Workplace Violence Prevention

The Workplace Violence Prevention Training is offered as a Basic and Instructor level course for private corporations, healthcare, security companies and any agency wanting to educate, prevent and mitigate the risk of violence to their employees.

www.AVADEtraining.com

Multiple training options for your organization:

- 2 hr. Intro Courses
- 1/2 Day Training Sessions
- One & Two Day Classes

AVADE® Personal Safety Training

Is a training program on how to increase your overall safety in all environments. The curriculum is based David Fowler's book, *Be Safe Not Sorry: the Art and Science of keeping YOU and your Family safe from crime and violence.*

Defensive Tactics Training System

This training program covers basic defensive tactics control techniques and defensive interventions. Course includes stance, movement, escort techniques, blocking, active defense skills, handgun retention and much more.

OC Pepper Spray Training

Tactical and Practical concepts of when and how to use pepper spray in a variety of environmental situations. Aerosol Pepper is a great less-than-lethal control and defense option for agencies that encounter aggression.

Handcuffs and Restraint Techniques

Training in the use of temporary metallic and plastic human restraints. Standing, kneeling and prone handcuffing techniques are covered. In this training course you will also learn searching, nomenclature, manufacture recommendations, drawing techniques and more...

AVADE®
Workplace Violence Prevention

Index

21961599R00091

Made in the USA
Charleston, SC
07 September 2013